FIND OUT ABOUT

ANCIENT EGYPT

What life was like in the ancient world

Philip Steele

Consultant: Felicity Cobbing

southwater

This edition published by Southwater

Distributed in the UK by The Manning Partnership
251-253 London Road East, Batheaston
Bath BA1 7RL
UK
tel. (0044) 01225 852 727
fax. (0044) 01225 852 852

Distributed in the USA by
Ottenheimer Publishing
5 Park Center Court
Suite 300
Owing Mills MD 2117-5001
USA
tel. (001) 410 902 9100
fax. (001) 410 902 7210

Distributed in Australia by
Sandstone Publishing
Unit 1, 360 Norton Street
Leichhardt
New South Wales 2040
Australia
tel. (0061) 2 9560 7888
fax. (0061) 2 9560 7488

Distributed in New Zealand
by
Five Mile Press NZ
PO Box 33-1071
Takapuna, Auckland 9
New Zealand
tel. (0064) 9 486 1925
fax. (0064) 9 486 1454

Southwater is an imprint of Anness Publishing Limited
© 1997, 2000 Anness Publishing Limited

1 3 5 7 9 10 8 6 4 2

Publisher: Joanna Lorenz
Senior Editor: Nicole Pearson
Designer: Simon Borrough
Illustration: Stuart Carter
Photography: John Freeman
Stylist: Thomasina Smith

Anness Publishing would like to thank the following
children for modelling for this book: Donna Marie
Bradley, Aslom Hussain, Alex Lindblom-Smith, Rajiv
M. Pattani, Emily Preddie, Brendan Scott and Harriet
Woollard. Gratitude also to their parents, Johanna
Primary and Walnut Tree Walk Schools.

Printed and bound in Hong Kong

PICTURE CREDITS
b=bottom, t-top, c=centre,
l=left, r=right
The Ancient Art and Architecture
Collection Ltd: pages 4b, 9tc, 10t, 10b, 11bc, 11tr, 12r, 12/13,
14br, 16, 17bl, 18l, 18r, 19tl, 20t, 21cl, 21br, 22b, 30l, 32r,
33tl, 36t, 37t, 38b, 39bc, 40l, 40t, 41b, 42r, 43r, 44br, 45tl,
45tr, 45b, 46t, 47t, 50/51, 52r, 53tr, 54tr, 56b, 57l, 58l and
59r; Copyright British Museum: pages 13t, 17tr, 19br, 20b,
28l, 28r, 30r, 35bc, 36bl, 38t, 39tr, 43l, 50l, 54br, 55l, 55br
and 57r; Peter Clayton: pages 15t, 15b, 19bl, 35bl, 35br,
36br, 44t, 44bl, 53tl, 53bl, 54l, 55tr and 60; C. M. Dixon:

CONTENTS

pages 8tr, 8b, 9b, 14t, 17tl, 21tr, 31tr, 34, 35t, 39tl, 47b, 48l,
48r, 51, 52l and 61t; Griffith Institute, Ashmolean Museum:
pages 4t, 27t and 27b; Michael Holford Photographs: pages
14bl, 29bl, 56t and 61b; Manchester Museum: page 29tl; Mary
Evans Picture Library: pages 24r, 24l and 32l; Bob Partridge and
the Ancient Egypt Picture Library: pages 19tr, 22t, 49t and 49br;
Courtesy of the Petrie Museum of Egyptian Archaeology,
University College London: page 41c; Radiotimes Hulton Picture
Library: page 46b; Zefa: pages 5r, 8tl, 9tl, 9tr, 11tl, 12l, 13b,
22l, 23t, 23b, 26, 26/27, 27c, 29tr, 31b, 33tr, 33cr, 33b, 40/41,
42l, 50r, 58r, 59l.

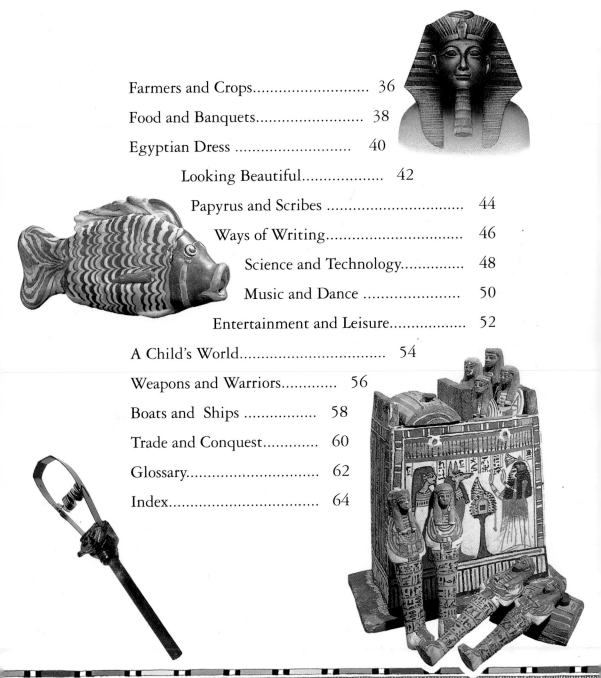

The Kingdom on the Nile

HORUS' EYE
This symbol can be seen on many Egyptian artefacts. It is the eye of the god Horus.

E GYPT IS A COUNTRY at the crossroads of Africa, Europe and Asia. If you could step back in time 5,000 years, you would discover an amazing civilization – the kingdom of the ancient Egyptians.

Most of Egypt is made up of baking hot, sandy deserts. These are crossed by the river Nile as it snakes its way north to the Mediterranean Sea. Every year, floods cover the banks of the Nile with mud. Plants grow well in this rich soil, and 8,000 years ago farmers were planting crops here. Wealth from farming led to trade and to the building of towns. By 3100BC a great kingdom had grown up in Egypt, ruled by royal families.

Ancient Egypt existed for over 3,000 years, longer even than the Roman Empire. Pyramids, temples and artefacts survive from this period to show us what life was like in the land of the pharaohs.

AMAZING DISCOVERIES
In 1922, the English archaeologist Howard Carter made an amazing discovery. He found the tomb of the young pharaoh Tutankhamun. No single find in Egypt has ever provided as much evidence as the discovery of this well-preserved tomb.

LIFE BY THE NILE
Tomb paintings show us how people lived in ancient Egypt. Here people water and harvest their crops, using water from the river Nile.

TIMELINE 6000BC–2000BC

The kingdom of ancient Egypt existed for over 3,000 years. The most successful periods of Egyptian power are known as the Old Kingdom, the Middle Kingdom and the New Kingdom.

wheat

sheep

boat with sail

c6000BC
Early people settle in the fertile Nile valley. They grow wheat and barley.

c5020–4500BC
Craftsmen make clay figures and fine pottery vessels. They also carve objects from ivory.

c4800BC
Farmers keep sheep, cattle and other animals.

c4000BC
Sails are used on Egyptian ships for the first time.

6000BC	5500BC	5000BC	4500BC	4000BC

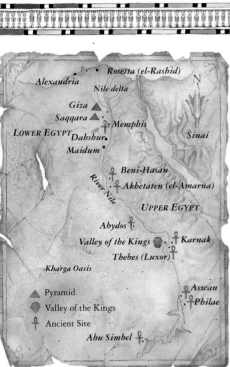

THE KINGDOM OF EGYPT

This map of Egypt today shows where there were important cities and sites in ancient times. The ancient Egyptians lived mostly along the banks of the river Nile and in the green, fertile lands of the delta. Through the ages, the Egyptians built many imposing temples in honour of their gods and mysterious tombs to house their dead. Most of these temples and tombs were built close to the major cities of Memphis and Thebes.

SURVIVORS OF THE DESERT

The face of the great pharaoh Ramesses II stares out at us. Huge statues of Ramesses were part of a temple cut from the rock face at Abu Simbel in 1269BC. During the 1960s the statues had to be raised because a new dam at Aswan turned this part of the Nile into a lake. Temples, tombs and statues such as those at Abu Simbel have survived for thousands of years in the dry desert heat. More recently, many monuments have started to disintegrate because of the polluted air around modern cities such as Luxor.

c4000–3500BC Reed shrines are built.

The first buildings are made from mud brick.

Craftsmen paint the first wall paintings and make stone statues.

one of over 750 hieroglyphic symbols in the Egyptian writing system

c3400BC Walled towns are built in Egypt.

3100BC The first of the great royal families govern Egypt. The Early Dynastic period begins.

King Narmer unites Egypt. He creates a capital at Memphis.

Egyptians use hieroglyphs.

2686BC Old Kingdom period.

2667BC Zoser becomes pharaoh.

2650BC Stepped pyramid built at Saqqara.

Stepped Pyramid

2600BC Pyramid built at Maidum.

2589BC Khufu becomes pharaoh. He later builds the Great Pyramid at Giza.

Great Sphinx

c2500BC Khafra, son of Khufu, dies. During his reign the Great Sphinx was built at Giza.

2181BC The Old Kingdom comes to an end.

The Intermediate Period begins. Minor kings in power.

4000BC   3500BC   3000BC   2500BC   2000BC

A Great Civilization

THE STORY of ancient Egypt began about 8,000 years ago when farmers started to plant crops and raise animals in the Nile Valley. By about 3400BC the Egyptians were building walled towns. Soon after that the northern part of the country (Lower Egypt) was united with the lands upstream (Upper Egypt) to form one country under a single king. The capital of this new kingdom was established at Memphis.

The first great period of Egyptian civilization is called the Old Kingdom. It lasted from 2686BC to 2181BC. This was when the pharaohs built great pyramids, the massive pointed tombs that still stand in the desert today.

During the Middle Kingdom (2050–1786BC), the capital was moved to the southern city of Thebes. The Egyptians gained control of Nubia and extended the area of land being farmed. Despite this period of success, the rule of the royal families of ancient Egypt was sometimes interrupted by disorder. In 1663BC, control of the country fell into foreign hands. The Hyksos, a group of Asian settlers, ruled Egypt for almost 100 years.

In 1567BC the Hyksos were overthrown by the princes of Thebes. The Thebans established the New Kingdom. This was the highest point of Egyptian civilization. Traders and soldiers travelled into Africa, Asia and the lands of the Mediterranean. However, by 525BC, the might of the Egyptians was coming to an end and Egypt became part of the Persian Empire. In 332BC rule passed to the Greeks. Finally, in 30BC, conquest was complete as Egypt fell under the control of the Roman Empire.

AFRICA

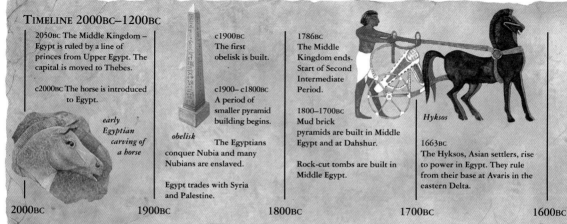

TIMELINE 2000BC–1200BC

2050BC The Middle Kingdom – Egypt is ruled by a line of princes from Upper Egypt. The capital is moved to Thebes.

c2000BC The horse is introduced to Egypt.

early Egyptian carving of a horse

c1900BC The first obelisk is built.

obelisk

c1900–c1800BC A period of smaller pyramid building begins.

The Egyptians conquer Nubia and many Nubians are enslaved.

Egypt trades with Syria and Palestine.

1786BC The Middle Kingdom ends. Start of Second Intermediate Period.

1800–1700BC Mud brick pyramids are built in Middle Egypt and at Dahshur.

Rock-cut tombs are built in Middle Egypt.

Hyksos

1663BC The Hyksos, Asian settlers, rise to power in Egypt. They rule from their base at Avaris in the eastern Delta.

2000BC   1900BC   1800BC   1700BC   1600BC

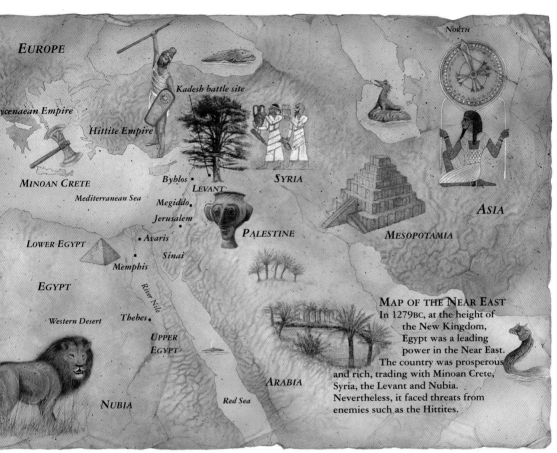

EUROPE

Mycenaean Empire

Hittite Empire

Kadesh battle site

NORTH

MINOAN CRETE

Mediterranean Sea

Byblos

LEVANT

Megiddo

Jerusalem

Avaris

Sinai

LOWER EGYPT

Memphis

SYRIA

PALESTINE

MESOPOTAMIA

ASIA

EGYPT

River Nile

Western Desert

Thebes

UPPER
EGYPT

NUBIA

ARABIA

Red Sea

MAP OF THE NEAR EAST
In 1279BC, at the height of
the New Kingdom,
Egypt was a leading
power in the Near East.
The country was prosperous
and rich, trading with Minoan Crete,
Syria, the Levant and Nubia.
Nevertheless, it faced threats from
enemies such as the Hittites.

Akhenaten

c1567BC The Hyksos are
defeated by Egyptians from the
southern city of Thebes.

1550BC The New Kingdom is
founded. Royal tombs are
built in the Valley of the
Kings.

1525BC Amenhotep
becomes pharaoh.

1500BC A village is
founded at Deir el-
Medina, near the
Valley of the Kings.

1498BC Queen Hatshepsut
rules as co-regent with the
child king Thutmose III.

1483BC Hatshepsut dies.

1478BC The rebellious
prince of Kadesh
is defeated by
Thutmose III at the
Battle of Megiddo in
the Near East.

*the cartouche of
Tutankhamun*

Thutmose III

1379BC
Akhenaten
introduces
worship of the
Sun god, Aten, as
the only religion.
A new capital is
established at el-Amarna.

c1334BC Smenkhkare,
Akhenaten's successor, moves
the capital back to Memphis.

1325BC Tutankhamun
is buried in the Valley
of the Kings.

1291BC
Seti I comes to power. He
builds the Hypostyle Hall at
Karnak.

1279BC
Ramesses II
becomes
pharaoh.

Ramesses II

1274BC
Ramesses II fights the Hittites
at the battle of Kadesh.

1600BC   1500BC   1400BC   1300BC   1200BC

Famous Pharaohs

FOR THOUSANDS OF YEARS ancient Egypt was ruled by royal families. We know much about the pharaohs and queens from these great dynasties because of their magnificent tombs and the public monuments raised in their honour.

Egypt's first ruler was King Narmer, who united the country in about 3100BC. Later pharaohs such as Zoser and Khufu are remembered for the great pyramids they had built as their tombs.

Pharaohs usually succeeded to the throne through royal birth. However, in some cases military commanders such as Horemheb came to power. Although Egypt's rulers were traditionally men, a few powerful women were made pharaoh. The most famous of these is the Greek queen Cleopatra, who ruled Egypt in 51BC.

KHAFRA
(reigned 2558–2532BC)
Khafra is the son of the pharaoh Khufu. He is remembered for his splendid tomb, the Second Pyramid at Giza and the Great Sphinx that guards it.

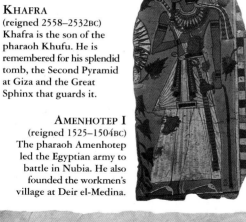

AMENHOTEP I
(reigned 1525–1504BC)
The pharaoh Amenhotep led the Egyptian army to battle in Nubia. He also founded the workmen's village at Deir el-Medina.

HATSHEPSUT
(reigned 1498–1483BC)
Hatshepsut was the half-sister and wife of Thutmose II. When her husband died, she was appointed to rule Egypt until her young stepson Thutmose III was old enough. However Queen Hatshepsut was ambitious and had herself crowned pharaoh. Hatshepsut is famous for her trading expeditions to the land of Punt. The walls of her temple at Deir el-Bahri show these exotic trips.

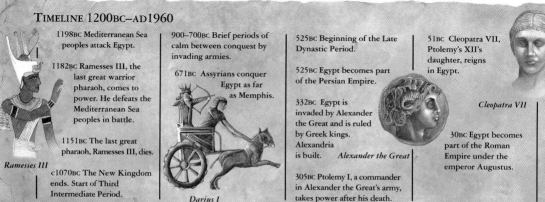

TIMELINE 1200BC–AD1960

1198BC Mediterranean Sea peoples attack Egypt.

1182BC Ramesses III, the last great warrior pharaoh, comes to power. He defeats the Mediterranean Sea peoples in battle.

1151BC The last great pharaoh, Ramesses III, dies.

Ramesses III

c1070BC The New Kingdom ends. Start of Third Intermediate Period.

900–700BC Brief periods of calm between conquest by invading armies.

671BC Assyrians conquer Egypt as far as Memphis.

Darius I

525BC Beginning of the Late Dynastic Period.

525BC Egypt becomes part of the Persian Empire.

332BC Egypt is invaded by Alexander the Great and is ruled by Greek kings. Alexandria is built. *Alexander the Great*

305BC Ptolemy I, a commander in Alexander the Great's army, takes power after his death.

51BC Cleopatra VII, Ptolemy's XII's daughter, reigns in Egypt.

Cleopatra VII

30BC Egypt becomes part of the Roman Empire under the emperor Augustus.

1200BC   900BC   600BC   300BC   AD0

TUTANKHAMUN
(reigned 1334–1325BC)
This pharaoh came to the throne when he was only nine years old. He died at the age of 18. Tutankhamun is remembered for his tomb in the Valley of the Kings, which was packed with amazing treasure.

THUTMOSE III
(reigned 1479–1425BC)
Thutmose III is remembered as a brave warrior king. He launched many military campaigns against the Syrians in the Near East. Records from the time tell of Thutmose marching fearlessly into battle at the head of his army, unconcerned about his own safety. He won a famous victory at Megiddo and then later at Kadesh. Thutmose III was buried in the Valley of the Kings.

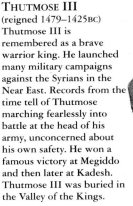

AKHENATEN
(reigned 1379–1334BC)
The Egyptians believed in many gods. However, when Akhenaten came to power, he introduced worship of one god, the Sun disc Aten. He moved the capital from Memphis to Akhetaten (now known as el-Amarna). His chief wife was the beautiful Queen Nefertiti.

RAMESSES II
(reigned 1279–1212BC)
One of the most famous pharaohs of all, Ramesses II, was the son of Seti I. He built many fine temples and defeated the Hittites at the Battle of Kadesh in 1274BC. The chief queen of Ramesses was Nefertari. Carvings of this graceful queen can be seen on Ramesses II's temple at Abu Simbel. Ramesses lived a long life and died at the age of 92. He was buried in the Valley of the Kings.

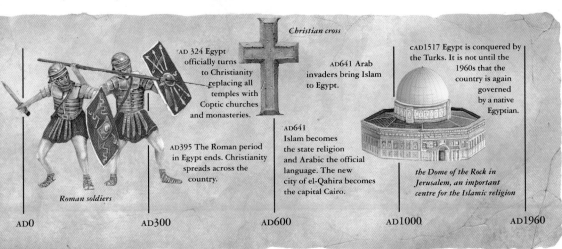

Christian cross

AD 324 Egypt officially turns to Christianity replacing all temples with Coptic churches and monasteries.

AD641 Arab invaders bring Islam to Egypt.

cAD1517 Egypt is conquered by the Turks. It is not until the 1960s that the country is again governed by a native Egyptian.

AD395 The Roman period in Egypt ends. Christianity spreads across the country.

AD641 Islam becomes the state religion and Arabic the official language. The new city of el-Qahira becomes the capital Cairo.

the Dome of the Rock in Jerusalem, an important centre for the Islamic religion

Roman soldiers

AD0   AD300   AD600   AD1000   AD1960

The Land of the Gods

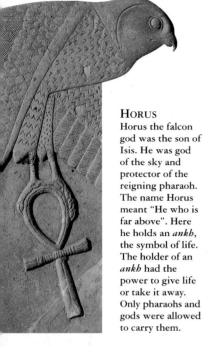

THE ANCIENT EGYPTIANS believed that the ordered world in which they lived had been created out of nothingness. Chaos and darkness could return at any time if the proper religious rituals were not followed. The spirit of the gods lived inside the pharaohs, who were honoured as god-kings. They looked after the everyday world for the gods. Over 2,000 gods were worshipped in ancient Egypt. Many gods were linked to a particular region. The mighty Amun was the god of Thebes. Some gods appeared as animals – Sebek the water god was a crocodile. Gods were also connected with jobs and interests. The hippopotamus goddess, Tawaret, looked after babies and childbirth.

Many ordinary Egyptians understood little about the religion of the court and nobles. They believed in magic, local spirits and superstitions.

HORUS
Horus the falcon god was the son of Isis. He was god of the sky and protector of the reigning pharaoh. The name Horus meant "He who is far above". Here he holds an *ankh*, the symbol of life. The holder of an *ankh* had the power to give life or take it away. Only pharaohs and gods were allowed to carry them.

LOTUS FLOWER
The lotus was a very important flower to the Egyptians. This sacred symbol was used to represent Upper Egypt.

THE GODDESS NUT
Nut, covered in stars, was goddess of the heavens. She is often shown with her body stretched across the sky. The Egyptians believed that Nut swallowed the Sun each evening and gave birth to it the next morning. She was married to the Earth god, Geb, and gave birth to the gods Isis and Osiris.

AMUN OF THEBES
Amun was originally the god of the city of Thebes. He later became popular throughout Egypt as the god of creation. By the time of the New Kingdom, Amun was combined with other powerful gods such as Ra, god of the Sun, and became known as Amun-Ra. He was believed to be the most powerful god of all. Amun is sometimes shown as a ram.

HOLY BEETLES
Scarabs are beetles that were sacred to the ancient Egyptians. Pottery or stone scarabs were used as lucky charms, seals, or as ring decorations. The base of these scarabs was often inscribed with stories telling of some great event.

OSIRIS, KING OF THE UNDERWORLD
The great god Osiris stands dressed as a king. He was one of the most important gods in ancient Egypt, the master of life and the spirit world. He was also the god of farming. Egyptian tales told how Osiris was murdered and cut into pieces by his brother Seth, the god of chaos. Anubis, the jackal-headed god of embalming, gathered the pieces together and his sister, Isis, brought Osiris back to life.

CAT MUMMIES
The Egyptians worshipped gods in the forms of animals from the Old Kingdom onwards. The cat goddess Bastet was said to be the daughter of the great Sun god, Ra. Cats were so holy to the Egyptians that at one time many of them were embalmed, wrapped in linen bandages and preserved as mummies. It is thought that bronze cat figures and these mummified cats were left as offerings to Bastet at her temple.

MIW THE CAT
Cats were holy animals in ancient Egypt. They even had their own god! The Egyptians' love of cats dated back to the early farmers who tamed cats to protect stores of grain from mice. Cats soon became popular pets. The Egyptian word for cat was *miw*, which was rather like a mew or miaow!

Priest, Politician and God

These emblems of the god Osiris became badges of royal authority. The crook stood for kingship and the flail for the fertility of the land.

flail

crook

THE WORD PHARAOH comes from the Egyptian *per-aa*, which meant great house or palace. It later came to mean the man who lived in the palace, the ruler. Pictures and statues show pharaohs with special badges of royalty, such as crowns, headcloths, false beards, sceptres and a crook and flail held in each hand.

The pharaoh was the most important person in Egypt. As a god-ruler, he was the link between the people and their gods. He therefore had to be protected and cared for. The pharaoh led a busy life. He was the high priest, the chief law-maker, the commander of the army and in charge of the country's wealth. He had to be a clever politician, too. The ancient Egyptians believed that on his death, the pharaoh became a god in his own right.

Pharaohs were generally men, but queens sometimes ruled Egypt if the pharaoh was too young. A pharaoh could take several wives. Within royal families it was common for fathers to marry daughters and for brothers to marry sisters. Sometimes pharaohs married foreign princesses in order to make an alliance with another country.

MOTHER GODDESS OF THE PHARAOHS

Hathor was worshipped as the mother goddess of each pharaoh. Here she is shown welcoming the pharaoh Horemheb to the afterlife. Horemheb was a nobleman who became a brilliant military commander. He was made pharaoh in 1323BC.

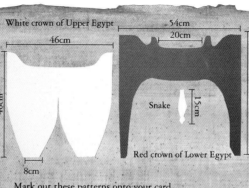

MAKE A CROWN

You will need: *2 sheets of A1 card (red and white), pencil, ruler, scissors, masking tape, cardboard roll, bandage, pva glue and brush, acrylic paint (white, gold), brush, beads, skewer, water pot and brush.*

White crown of Upper Egypt

46cm

40cm

8cm

Mark out these patterns onto your card. Cut around them with scissors.

54cm

20cm

Snake

15cm

55cm

Red crown of Lower Egypt

1 Bend the shape made from the white card into a cylinder, as shown. Use lengths of masking tape to join the two edges together firmly.

RAMESSES MEETS THE GODS

This painting shows the dead pharaoh Ramesses I meeting the gods Horus (left) and Anubis (right). Pharaohs had to pass safely through the after-life or the link between the gods and the world would be broken forever.

THE QUEEN'S TEMPLE

This great temple (*below*) was built in honour of Queen Hatshepsut. It lies at the foot of towering cliffs at Deir el-Bahri, on the west bank of the Nile near the Valley of the Kings. The queen had the temple built as a place for her body to be prepared for burial. Pyramids, tombs and temples were important symbols of power in Egypt. By building this temple, Hatshepsut wanted people to remember her as a pharaoh in her own right.

HATSHEPSUT

A female pharaoh was so unusual that pictures of Queen Hatshepsut show her with all the badges of a male king, including a false beard! Here she wears the pharaoh's crown. The cobra on the front of the crown is the badge of Lower Egypt.

The double crown worn by the pharaohs was called the pschent. *It symbolized the unification of the two kingdoms. The white section at the top* (hedjet) *stood for Upper Egypt, and the red section at the bottom* (deshret) *for Lower Egypt.*

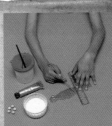

2 Tape a cardboard roll into the hole at the top. Plug its end with a ball of bandage. Then tape the bandage in position and glue down the edges.

3 Wrap the white section with lengths of bandage. Paint over these with an equal mixture of white paint and glue. Leave the crown in a warm place to dry.

4 Now take the shape made from the red card. Wrap it tightly around the white section, as shown, joining the edges with masking tape.

5 Now paint the snake gold, sticking on beads as eyes. When dry, score lines across its body. Bend the snake's body and glue it to the crown, as shown.

13

Court and Nobles

EGYPTIAN PALACES were vast complexes. They included splendid public buildings where the pharaoh would meet foreign rulers and carry out important ceremonies. Members of the royal family lived in luxury in beautiful townhouses with painted walls and tiled floors near the palace.

The governors of Egypt's regions also lived like princes, and pharaohs had to be careful that they did not become too rich and powerful. The royal court included large numbers of officials and royal advisors. There were lawyers, architects, tax officials, priests and army officers. The most important court official of all was the vizier, who carried out many of the pharaoh's duties for him.

The officials and nobles were at the top of Egyptian society. But most of the hard work that kept the country running smoothly was carried out by merchants and craft workers, by farmers, labourers and slaves.

GREAT LADIES
Ahmose-Nefertari was the wife of Ahmose I. She carries a lotus flower and a flail. Kings could take many wives and it was also common for them to have a harem of beautiful women.

A NOBLEMAN AND HIS WIFE
This limestone statue shows an unknown couple from Thebes. The man may have worked in a well-respected profession, as a doctor, government official, or engineer. Noblewomen did not work but were quite independent. Any property that a wife brought into her marriage remained hers.

THE SPLENDOURS OF THE COURT
This is the throne room of Ramesses III's palace at Medinet Habu, on the west bank of the Nile near Thebes. Pharaohs often had many palaces and Medinet Habu was one of Ramesses III's lesser ones. Surviving fragments of tiles and furniture give us an idea of just how splendid the royal court must have been. A chamber to one side of the throne room is even believed to be an early version of a shower cubicle!

RELAXATION

Ankherhau (*above*), a wealthy overseer of workmen, relaxes at home with his wife. They are listening to a harpist. Life was pleasant for those who could afford it. Kings and nobles had dancers, musicians and acrobats to entertain them. Cooks worked in their kitchens preparing sumptuous meals. By comparison, ordinary people ate simple food, rarely eating meat except for the small animals they caught themselves.

HAIR CARE

The royal family was waited on by domestic servants who attended to their every need. Here (*left*), the young Queen Kawit, wife of the pharaoh Mentuhotep II, has her hair dressed by her personal maid. Although many of the female servants employed in wealthy households were slaves, a large number of servants were free. This meant that they had the right to leave their employer at any time.

Towns, Homes and Gardens

THE GREAT CITIES of ancient Egypt, such as Memphis and Thebes, were built along the banks of the river Nile. Small towns grew up haphazardly around them. Special workmen's towns such as Deir el-Medina were also set up around major burial sites and temples to help with building work.

Egyptian towns were defended by thick walls and the streets were planned on a grid pattern. The straight dirt roads had a stone drainage channel, or gutter, running down the middle. Parts of the town housed important officials, while other parts were home to craft workers and poor labourers.

Only temples were built to last. They were made of stone. Mud brick was used to construct all other buildings from royal palaces to workers' dwellings. Most Egyptian homes had roofs supported with palm logs and floors made of packed earth. In the homes of wealthier Egyptians, walls were sometimes plastered and painted. The rooms of their houses included bedrooms, living rooms, kitchens in thatched courtyards and workshops. Homes were furnished with beds, chairs, stools and benches. In the cool of the evenings people would sit on the flat roofs or walk and talk in cool, shady gardens.

THE GARDEN OF NAKHT
The royal scribe Nakht and his wife Tjiui take an evening stroll through their garden. Trees and shrubs surround a peaceful pool. Egyptian gardens included date palms, pomegranates, grape vines, scarlet poppies and blue and pink lotus flowers. Artists in ancient Egypt showed objects in the same picture from different angles, so the trees around Nakht's pool are flattened out.

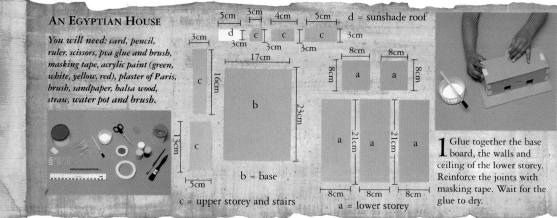

AN EGYPTIAN HOUSE

You will need: card, pencil, ruler, scissors, pva glue and brush, masking tape, acrylic paint (green, white, yellow, red), plaster of Paris, brush, sandpaper, balsa wood, straw, water pot and brush.

d = sunshade roof

b = base

c = upper storey and stairs

a = lower storey

1 Glue together the base board, the walls and ceiling of the lower storey. Reinforce the joints with masking tape. Wait for the glue to dry.

ABOVE THE FLOODS

The homes of wealthy people were often built on platforms to stop damp passing through the mud brick walls. This also raised it above the level of any possible flood damage.

SOUL HOUSES

Pottery models give us a good idea of how the homes of poorer Egyptians looked. During the Middle Kingdom, these soul houses were left as tomb offerings. The Egyptians placed food in the courtyard of the house to feed the person's soul after death.

MUD BRICK

The Egyptians made mud bricks from the thick clay soil left behind by the Nile floods. The clay was taken to the brickyard and mixed with water, pebbles and chopped straw. Mud brick is still used as a building material for houses in Egypt today and is made in the same way.

straw

mud

BRICK MAKING

A group of labourers make bricks. First mud was collected in leather buckets and taken to the building site. There, it was mixed with straw and pebbles. Finally the mixture was put into a mould. At this stage, bricks were sometimes stamped with the name of the pharaoh or the building for which they were made. They were then left to dry in the hot sunshine for several days, before being carried away in a sling.

Egyptian houses had a large main room that opened directly onto the street. In many homes, stairs led up to the roof. People would often sleep there during very hot weather.

2 Now glue together the top storey and stairs. Again, use masking tape to reinforce the joints. When the top storey is dry, glue it to the lower storey.

3 Glue the balsa pillars into the front of the top storey. When the house is dry, cover it in wet paste of plaster of Paris. Paint the pillars red or a colour of your choice.

4 Paint the whole building a dried mud colour. Next paint a green strip along the side. Use masking tape to ensure straight edges. Sand any rough edges.

5 Now make a shelter for the rooftop. Use four balsa struts as supports. The roof can be made of card glued with straw. Glue the shelter into place.

Skilled Workers

IN ANCIENT EGYPT, skilled workers formed a middle class between the poor labourers and the rich officials and nobles. Wall paintings and models show us craft workers carving stone or wood, making pottery, or working precious metals. There were boat builders and chariot makers, too.

Artists and craft workers could be well rewarded for their skills, and some became famous for their work. The house and workshops of a sculptor called Thutmose was excavated in el-Amarna in 1912. He was very successful in his career and was a favourite of the royal family.

Craft workers often lived in their own part of town. A special village was built at Deir el-Medina, near Thebes, for the builders of the magnificent, but secret, royal tombs. Among the 100 or so houses there, archaeologists found delivery notes for goods, sketches and plans drawn on broken pottery. Working conditions cannot always have been very good, for records show that the workers once went on strike. They may well have helped to rob the tombs that they themselves had built.

GLASS IN GOLD
This pendant shows the skill of Egyptian craft workers. It is in the form of Nekhbet the vulture, goddess of Upper Egypt. Glass of many colours has been set in solid gold using a technique called cloisonné. Like many other such beautiful objects, it was found in the tomb of Tutankhamun.

JEWELLERS AT WORK
Jewellers are shown at their work benches in this wall painting from 1395BC. One is making an ornamental collar while the others are working with precious stones or beads. The bow strings are being used to power metal drill bits.

A HIVE OF INDUSTRY

Skilled craftsmen are hard at work in this bustling workshop. Carpenters are sawing and drilling wood, potters are painting pottery jars, and masons are chiselling stone. A foreman would inspect the quality of each finished item.

DEIR EL-MEDINA

The stone foundations of the village of Deir el-Medina may still be seen on the west bank of the Nile. They are about 3,500 years old. In its day, Deir el-Medina housed the skilled workers who built and decorated the royal tombs in the Valley of the Kings. The men worked for eight days out of ten. The village existed for four centuries and was large and prosperous. Nevertheless, the workmen's village did not have its own water supply, so water had to be carried to the site and stored in a guarded tank.

SURVEYING THE LAND

Officials stretch a cord across a field to calculate its area. These men have been employed to survey an estate for government records.

bow drill

saw

pull saw

axe

chisel

bradawl

oil flask

smoothing stone

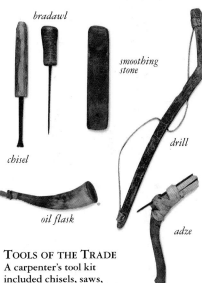

drill

adze

TOOLS OF THE TRADE

A carpenter's tool kit included chisels, saws, mallets, axes and knives. Bradawls were also used for making starter holes before drilling. The tools were generally made of wood and copper. Carpenters made fine chairs, beds, chests, boxes and beautiful coffins with these sophisticated tools.

Arts and Crafts

THE ANCIENT EGYPTIANS loved beautiful objects, and the craft items that have survived still amaze us today. There are shining gold rings and pendants, necklaces inlaid with glass and a dazzling blue pottery called faience. Jars made of a smooth white stone called alabaster have been preserved in almost perfect condition, along with chairs and chests made of cedar wood imported from the Near East.

Egyptians made beautiful baskets and storage pots. Some pottery was made from river clay, but the finest pots were made from a chalky clay found at Quena. Pots were shaped by hand or, later, on a potter's wheel. Some were polished with a smooth pebble until their surface shone. We know so much about Egyptian craft work because many beautiful items were placed in tombs, so that the dead person could use them in the next world.

ALABASTER ART
This elaborate jar was among the treasures in the tomb of Tutankhamun. Jars such as this would have held precious oils and perfumes.

GLASS FISH
This beautiful stripy fish looks as if it should be swimming in the reefs of the Red Sea. In fact it is a glass jar used to store oils. Glass-making became popular in Egypt after 1500BC. The glass was made from sand and salty crystals. It would then have been coloured with metals and shaped while still hot.

MAKE A LOTUS TILE

You will need: card (2 sheets), pencil, ruler, scissors, self-drying clay, modelling tool, sandpaper acrylic paint (blue, gold, green, yellow ochre), water pot and brush. Optional: rolling pin & board.

1 Using the final picture as reference, draw both tile shapes onto card. Cut them out. Draw the whole pattern of tiles onto the sheet of card and cut around the border.

2 Roll out the clay on a board with a rolling pin or bottle. Place the overall outline over the clay and carefully trim off the edges. Discard the extra clay.

3 Mark the individual tile patterns into the clay, following the outlines carefully. Cut through the lines, but do not separate them out yet.

DESERT RICHES

The dwellers of the green Nile valley feared and disliked the desert. They called it the Red Land. However, the deserts did provide them with great mineral wealth, including blue-green turquoise, purple amethyst and blue agate.

blue agate   *turquoise*   *amethyst*

ROYAL TILES

Many beautiful tiles have been discovered by archaeologists. It is thought that they were used to decorate furniture and floors in the palaces of the Egyptian pharaohs.

TUTANKHAMUN'S WAR CHEST

This painted chest shows Tutankhamun in battle against the Syrians and the Nubians. On the lid, the young king is also seen hunting in the desert. The incredible detail of the painting shows that this was the work of a very skilled artist. When Tutankhamun's tomb was opened, the chest was found to contain children's clothes. The desert air was so dry that neither the wood, leather nor fabric had rotted.

NEKHBET COLLAR

This splendid collar was one of 17 found in Tutankhamun's tomb. The spectacular wings of the vulture goddess Nekhbet include 250 feather sections made of coloured glass set in gold. The vulture's beak and eye are made from a black, volcanic glass called obsidian. This and other amazing objects found in the young king's tomb show us the incredible skill of Egyptian craftsmen.

4 Now use the tool to score patterns of leaves and flowers into the surface of the soft clay, as shown. Separate the pieces and allow them to dry.

5 When one side of each tile has dried, turn it over. Leave the other side to dry. Then sand down the edges of the tiles until they are smooth.

6 The tiles are now ready for painting. Carefully paint the patterns in green, yellow ochre, gold and blue. Leave them in a warm place to dry.

These tiles are similar to those found at a royal palace in Thebes. The design looks rather like a lotus, the sacred waterlily of ancient Egypt.

The Pyramid Builders

THE PYRAMIDS were massive four-sided tombs, built for the pharaohs of the Old Kingdom. Each side, shaped like a triangle, met together in a point at the top. The first Egyptian pyramid was built at Saqqara in about 2650BC. It had stepped sides. The most impressive pyramids, built at Giza over 100 years later, had flat sides. The summit of each pyramid was probably capped in gold. Inside the pyramids were burial chambers and secret passages. No one really knows why the Egyptians built these tombs in pyramid shapes, but it may have been seen as a stairway to heaven to help the pharaoh achieve eternal life.

The pyramids were built with fantastic skill and mathematical accuracy by a team of architects, engineers and stonemasons. They still stand today. The manual labour was provided not by slaves, but by about 100,000 ordinary people. These unskilled workers had to offer their services each year when the flooding Nile made work in the fields impossible.

WORN DOWN BY THE WIND
This pyramid at Dahshur was built for pharaoh Amenemhat III. Once the limestone casing had been stolen, its mud-brick core was easily worn down by the harsh desert winds. Pyramids had become popular burial monuments after the building of the first step pyramid at Saqqara. Examples can be seen at Maidum, Dahshur and Giza. However, Amenemhat's pyramid is typical of those built during the Middle Kingdom when inferior materials were used.

THE STEP PYRAMID
The earliest step pyramid was built at Saqqara for the pharaoh Zoser. The tomb probably started out as a mastaba, an older type of burial site made up of a brick structure over an underground tomb. The upper levels of Zoser's mastaba were redesigned as a pyramid with six huge steps. It was 60m high and towered above the desert sands. It covered the underground tomb of the pharaoh and included 11 burial chambers for the other members of the royal family.

ROYAL ARCHITECT
Imhotep was vizier, or treasurer, in the court of the great pharaoh Zoser. He designed the huge step pyramid at Saqqara. This pyramid was the first large monument made entirely of stone. Imhotep was also a wise man who was an accomplished scribe, astronomer, doctor, priest and architect. In the late period of the Egyptian empire, he was worshipped as a god of medicine.

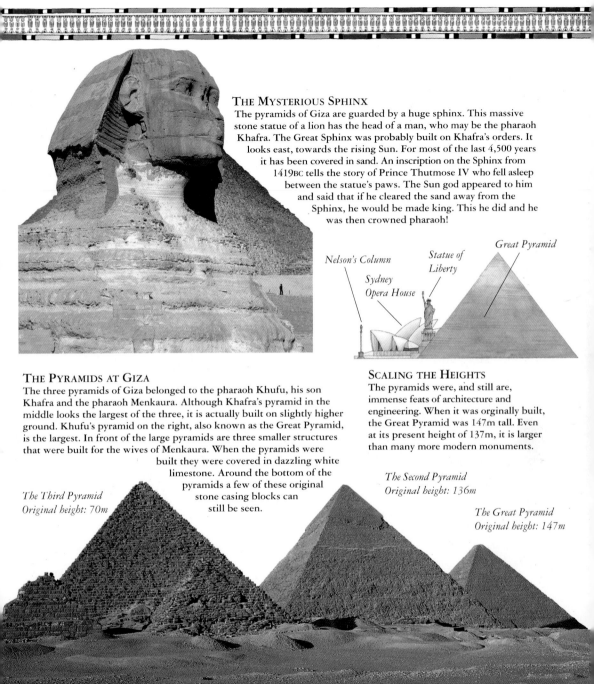

THE MYSTERIOUS SPHINX

The pyramids of Giza are guarded by a huge sphinx. This massive stone statue of a lion has the head of a man, who may be the pharaoh Khafra. The Great Sphinx was probably built on Khafra's orders. It looks east, towards the rising Sun. For most of the last 4,500 years it has been covered in sand. An inscription on the Sphinx from 1419BC tells the story of Prince Thutmose IV who fell asleep between the statue's paws. The Sun god appeared to him and said that if he cleared the sand away from the Sphinx, he would be made king. This he did and he was then crowned pharaoh!

Nelson's Column

Sydney Opera House

Statue of Liberty

Great Pyramid

THE PYRAMIDS AT GIZA

The three pyramids of Giza belonged to the pharaoh Khufu, his son Khafra and the pharaoh Menkaura. Although Khafra's pyramid in the middle looks the largest of the three, it is actually built on slightly higher ground. Khufu's pyramid on the right, also known as the Great Pyramid, is the largest. In front of the large pyramids are three smaller structures that were built for the wives of Menkaura. When the pyramids were built they were covered in dazzling white limestone. Around the bottom of the pyramids a few of these original stone casing blocks can still be seen.

SCALING THE HEIGHTS

The pyramids were, and still are, immense feats of architecture and engineering. When it was orginally built, the Great Pyramid was 147m tall. Even at its present height of 137m, it is larger than many more modern monuments.

The Second Pyramid
Original height: 136m

The Great Pyramid
Original height: 147m

The Third Pyramid
Original height: 70m

Wonder of the World

FOR MANY YEARS the Great Pyramid at Giza was the largest building in the world. Its base is about 230m square, and its original point was 147m high. It is made up of about 2,300,000 massive blocks of stone, each one weighing about 2.5 tonnes. It was the oldest of the seven ancient wonders of the world and is the only one left standing today. Even in ancient times, tourists came to marvel at the size of the Great Pyramid, and vast numbers of people still come to Giza today. The Great Pyramid is incredible in terms of both scale and age. It was built for the pharaoh Khufu, who died in 2566BC. Nearby was a great temple built in his honour. The purpose of the pyramid was to protect Khufu's body while he journeyed to meet the gods after his death. A 47m long passage leads to one of the three burial chambers inside the pyramid, but the pharaoh's body was never found in the tomb. It had been robbed long ago.

GRAND GALLERY
This steep passage is known as the Grand Gallery. It leads up to the burial chamber in the Great Pyramid. After King Khufu's funeral, granite blocks were slid down the gallery to seal off the chamber. However, ancient Egyptian tomb robbers still managed to break into the chamber and steal its contents.

MAKE A PYRAMID

You will need: card, pencil, ruler, scissors, pva glue and brush, masking tape, acrylic paint (yellow, white, gold), plaster paste, sandpaper, water pot and brush.

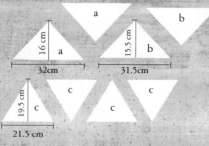

a   b

16 cm   a   15.5 cm   b

32cm   31.5cm

19.5 cm   c   c

21.5 cm

Make the pyramid in two halves. Cut out one triangle (a) for the base, one triangle (b) for the inside and two of triangle (c) for the sides of each half section.

1 Glue the half section of the pyramid together, binding the joints with pieces of masking tape, as shown. Now make the second half section in the same way.

24

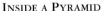

INSIDE A PYRAMID

This cross-section shows the inside of the Great Pyramid. The design of the interior changed several times during its construction. An underground chamber may originally have been intended as Khufu's burial place. This chamber was never finished. A second chamber, known as the Queen's Chamber, was also found empty. The pharaoh was actually buried in the King's Chamber. Once the funeral was over, the tomb had to be sealed from the inside. Blocks of stone were slid down the Grand Gallery. The workmen left through a shaft and along a corridor before the stones thudded into place.

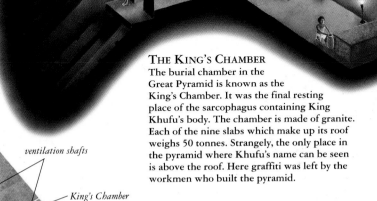

THE KING'S CHAMBER

The burial chamber in the Great Pyramid is known as the King's Chamber. It was the final resting place of the sarcophagus containing King Khufu's body. The chamber is made of granite. Each of the nine slabs which make up its roof weighs 50 tonnes. Strangely, the only place in the pyramid where Khufu's name can be seen is above the roof. Here graffiti was left by the workmen who built the pyramid.

ventilation shafts

King's Chamber

Grand Gallery

Queen's Chamber

escape shaft for workers

corridor

unfinished chamber

2 Mix up yellow and white paint with a little plaster paste to achieve a sandy texture. Then add a little glue so that it sticks to the card. Paint the pyramid sections.

3 Leave the painted pyramid sections to dry in a warm place. When they are completely dry, sand down the tips until they are smooth and mask them off with tape.

4 Now paint the tips of each half of the pyramid gold and leave to dry. Finally, glue the two halves together and place your pyramid on a bed of sand to display.

The building of the Great Pyramid probably took about 23 years. Originally the pyramids were cased in pale limestone, so they would have looked a brilliant white. The capstone at the very top of the pyramid was probably covered in gold.

The Valley of the Kings

IN 1550BC, the capital of Egypt moved south to Thebes. This marked the beginning of the New Kingdom. The ancient Egyptians no longer built pyramids as they were obvious targets for tomb robbers. The people still raised great temples to honour their dead rulers, but now the pharaohs were buried in secret underground tombs. These were hidden away in the cliffs bordering the desert on the west bank of the Nile, where the Sun set each night. It was from here that the pharaoh would journey to meet the Sun god on his death.

The burial sites near Thebes included the Valley of the Kings, the Valley of the Queens and the Valley of the Nobles. The tombs were packed with glittering treasure. Practical

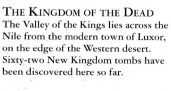

items that the pharaoh would need in the next life were buried there too, such as food, royal clothing, gilded furniture, jewellery, weapons and chariots.

The tombs were guarded by a secret police force and were designed with traps to foil any intruders. Even so, many sites were robbed in ancient times. Luckily, some remained unspoiled and have given archaeologists an amazing look into the world of ancient Egypt.

THE KINGDOM OF THE DEAD
The Valley of the Kings lies across the Nile from the modern town of Luxor, on the edge of the Western desert. Sixty-two New Kingdom tombs have been discovered here so far.

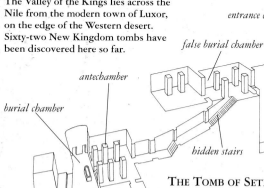

entrance corridor

false burial chamber

antechamber

burial chamber

shaft

hidden stairs

THE TOMB OF SETI I
One of the finest tombs in the Valley of the Kings belonged to the pharaoh Seti I, who died in 1279BC. Its splendid hall and burial chamber were protected by hidden shafts and stairs.

THE MASK
This beautiful mask was placed over the face of Tutankhamun's mummy. It presents the pharaoh in the image of the Sun god, Ra. This mask is made of solid gold and a blue stone called lapis lazuli. Tutankhamun's tomb was the most spectacular find in the Valley of the Kings. The inner chambers had not been disturbed for over 3,260 years.

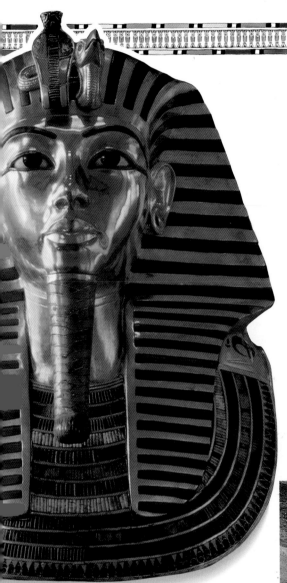

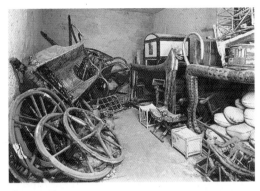

GRAVE ROBBERS

When Howard Carter entered the tomb of Tutankhamun, he discovered that robbers had reached its outer chambers in ancient times. The Valley guards had resealed the tomb, but many items were left in heaps and piles. This picture shows two chariots, two beds, a chest, stools and food boxes.

UNTOLD TREASURES

This gold perfume box was found in Tutankhamun's burial chamber. The oval-shaped designs are called cartouches. They contain pictures of the pharaoh as a boy.

WORKERS ON SITE

The excavations of the 1800s and 1900s brought teams of Egyptian workers back into the Valley of the Kings for the first time in thousands of years. They dug down into tombs, carried out soil in baskets and shifted rocks. This photograph was taken in 1922 during Howard Carter's excavations that uncovered the tomb of Tutankhamun.

Mummies and Coffins

THE EARLY EGYPTIANS found out that people buried in the desert were often preserved in the dry sand. Their bodies dried out and became mummified. Over the ages, the Egyptians became experts at preserving bodies by embalming them. They believed that the dead would need to use their bodies in the next life.

The methods of mummification varied over the years. The process usually took about 70 days. The brains were hooked out through the nose and the other organs were removed and placed in special jars. Only the heart was left so that it could be weighed in the next life. Embalming involved drying the body out with salty crystals of natron. Afterwards it was stuffed and covered with oils and ointments and then wrapped in bandages. The mummy was then placed inside a series of coffins in the shape of the body.

MUMMY CASE
This beautiful gold case contains the mummy of a priestess. Once the embalmed body had been wrapped in bandages it was placed in a richly decorated coffin. Both the inside and outside would be covered in spells to help the dead person in the underworld. Sometimes more than one coffin was used. The inner coffins would be of brightly painted or gilded wood (*as left*) and the outer coffin would be a stone sarcophagus.

CANOPIC JARS
Special jars were used to store the body's organs. The human-headed jar held the liver. The baboon jar contained the lungs. The stomach was put in the jackal-headed jar and finally the guts were placed in the falcon-headed jar.

CANOPIC JARS

You will need: self-drying clay, rolling pin and board, ruler, modelling tool, sandpaper, masking tape, acrylic paint (white, blue, green, yellow, black), water pot and brush.

1 Roll out ³/₄ of the clay and cut out a circle about 7cm in diameter. This is the base of the jar. Now roll out thin strips of clay. Coil these from the base to make the sides.

2 Carefully press out the bumps between the coils until the sides of the jar are smooth and round. Finally trim the top of the jar with a modelling tool.

3 Now make a lid for the jar. Measure the size needed and cut out a circle of the remaining clay. Mould it into a dome. Model the head of a baboon on to the lid.

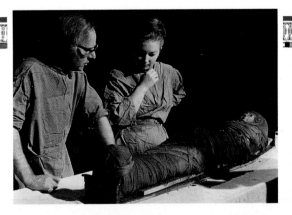

BENEATH THE BANDAGES

Unwrapping a mummy is a delicate operation. Today, archaeologists can use scanning or X-ray equipment to examine the mummies' bodies. It is possible to tell what food they once ate, the work they did and the illnesses they suffered from. X-rays also show the stuffing used to replace the internal organs.

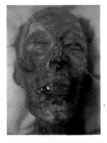

RAMESSES II

This is the unwrapped head of the mummy of Ramesses II. Wadding was placed in his eye sockets to stop the natron (preserving salts) from destroying his features.

It was believed that any part of a person's body could be used against them. For this reason the organs were removed and stored in canopic jars. Spells written on the jars protected them.

THE OPENING OF THE MOUTH CEREMONY

The last ritual before burial was led by a priest wearing the mask of the god Anubis. The human-shaped coffin was held upright and its face was touched with magical instruments. This ceremony enabled the mummy to speak, see and hear in the next world.

4 Hapy the baboon guarded the mummy's lungs. Use the modelling tool to make the baboon's eyes and long nose. Leave the lid in a warm place to dry.

5 When both the jar and the lid are completely dry, rub them down with sandpaper until they are smooth. The lid should fit snugly on to the jar.

6 It is now time to paint your jar. Use the masking tape to protect the baboon's face and to help you get the stripes straight. Follow the colours in the picture above.

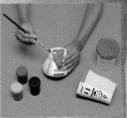

7 Paint hieroglyphs down the front of the jar as shown. Use the letters on page 46 to help you. The canopic jar is now ready for the funeral.

29

Egyptian Funerals

WHEN A PHARAOH died, everything possible was done to make sure he completed his journey to the gods in safety. During the New Kingdom, the ruler's coffin, containing his mummy, would be placed on a boat and ferried from Thebes to the west bank of the Nile. There it was placed in a shrine and hauled on a sled drawn by oxen to the Valley of the Kings. The funeral procession was spectacular.

Priests scattered offerings of milk and burned incense. Women played the part of official mourners, screaming and weeping. In front of the tomb there was dancing and a priest read out spells. After a ceremony and a banquet, the coffin was placed in the tomb with food, drink and treasure. The tomb was then sealed.

SHABTI FIGURES
Shabti were model figures placed in a tomb. Their purpose was to work for the dead person in the next life, acting as servants or labourers. They would be brought to life by a spell.

LIFE AFTER DEATH
The *ba*, or personality, of a dead person hovers over the mummy. It appears as a bird. Its job is to help the dead body rejoin its spirit, or *ka*, so it can live in the next world. This picture is taken from a papyrus called the Book of the Dead. This book acted as a guide to the after-life for the dead. It contained spells to guarantee safe passage through the underworld. Priests read from it at the funeral and then it was buried with the mummy.

MAKE AN UDJAT EYE
You will need: self-drying clay, modelling tool, sandpaper, acrylic paint (red, blue, black, white), water pot and brush. Optional: rolling pin & board.

1 Begin by rolling out the clay on the board. Use the modelling tool to cut in the pattern of the eye pieces. Refer to step 2 for the shape of each piece.

2 Remove all extra clay and arrange the eye pieces on the board. The eye is meant to represent the eye of the falcon-headed god Horus.

3 Next, press the pieces together until you have the full shape of the eye. Use the modelling tool if necessary. Now leave the eye to dry.

THE FUNERAL PROCESSION

The coffin lies inside a boat-shaped shrine on a sled. The priests chant and pray as they begin to haul the sled up towards the burial place. A burial site such as the Valley of the Kings is called a necropolis, which means 'the city of the dead'. The coffin would be taken into the tomb through a deep corridor to its final resting place. In the burial chamber, it would be surrounded by fine objects and riches.

FUNERARY BOAT

This beautiful model boat was placed in the tomb of Tutankhamun. It is made of alabaster and shows two female mourners who represent the goddess Isis and her sister Nephthys. They are mourning the death of the murdered god Osiris. Between them is an empty sarcophagus (stone coffin casing), which may once have been used to hold oils. Many other boats were found in the tomb. They were meant to carry the pharaoh after he had died, just as a boat had carried Ra, the Sun god, through *Dwat*, the underworld.

4 Smooth the surface with fine sandpaper. The eye of Horus is now ready for painting. Horus was said to have lost his eye in a battle with Seth, the god of Chaos.

5 Paint in the white of the eye and add the black eyebrow and pupil. Next, paint in the red liner. Finally, paint the rest of the eye charm blue and leave to dry.

When Horus lost his eye, it was made better by the goddess Hathor. Udjat meant making better. Charms like this were wrapped up with mummies to protect them in the next life.

Priests, Temples and Festivals

MASSIVE TEMPLES were built in honour of the Egyptian gods. Many can still be seen today. They have great pillars and massive gates, courtyards and avenues of statues. Once, these would have led to a shrine that was believed to be the home of a god.

Ordinary people did not gather to worship in an Egyptian temple as they might today in a church. Only priests were allowed in the temples. They carried out rituals on behalf of the pharaoh, making offerings of food, burning incense, playing music and singing. They had complicated rules about washing and shaving their heads, and some had to wear special clothes such as leopard skins. Noblewomen served as priestesses during some ceremonies. Many priests had little knowledge of religion and just served in the temple for three months before returning to their normal work. Other priests studied the stars and spells.

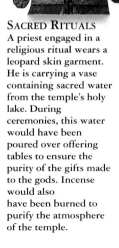

There were many religious festivals during which the god's shrine would be carried to other temples in a great procession. This was when ordinary Egyptians joined in worship. Offerings of food made to the gods were given back to the people for public feasting.

SACRED RITUALS
A priest engaged in a religious ritual wears a leopard skin garment. He is carrying a vase containing sacred water from the temple's holy lake. During ceremonies, this water would have been poured over offering tables to ensure the purity of the gifts made to the gods. Incense would also have been burned to purify the atmosphere of the temple.

KARNAK
This painting by David Roberts shows the massive temple of Karnak as it appeared in 1850. It still stands just outside the modern town of Luxor. The temple's most important god was Amun-Ra. The site also includes courts and buildings sacred to other gods and goddesses, including Mut (a vulture goddess, wife of Amun) and Khons (the Moon god, son of Amun). The Great Temple was enlarged and rebuilt over about 2,000 years.

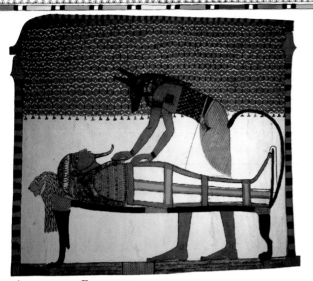

ANUBIS THE EMBALMER

A priest wears the mask of Anubis to embalm a body. This jackal-headed god was said to have prepared the body of the god Osiris for burial. He and his priests had strong links with mummies and the practice of embalming.

TEMPLE OF HORUS

A statue of Horus, the falcon god, guards the temple at Edfu. There was a temple on this site during the New Kingdom. However, the building that still stands today dates back to the period of Greek rule. This temple was dedicated to Horus and his wife, the cow goddess Hathor. Inside the temple there are stone carvings showing Horus fighting the enemies of Osiris, his father.

KALABSHA TEMPLE

The Kalabsha temple was one of the largest temples in Lower Nubia. In the 1960s, the Aswan Dam was built and Lower Nubia was flooded. Many monuments such as the temples at Abu Simbel and Philae had to be moved. The temple at Kalabsha was dismantled, and its 13,000 blocks of stone were moved to New Kalabsha, where it was rebuilt.

GATEWAY TO ISIS

The temple of Philae (*above*) was built in honour of Isis, the mother goddess. Isis was worshipped all over Egypt and in many other lands, too. Massive gateways called pylons guard the temple of Philae. Pylons guard the way to many Egyptian temples and were used for special ceremonies.

Workers and Slaves

THE PHARAOHS may have believed that it was their links with the gods that kept Egypt going, but really it was the hard work of the ordinary people. It was they who dug the soil, worked in the mines and quarries, sailed the boats on the river Nile, marched with the army into Syria or Nubia, cooked food and raised children.

Slavery was not very important in ancient Egypt, but it did exist. Most of the slaves were prisoners who had been captured during the many wars that Egypt fought with their neighbours in the Near East. Slaves were usually treated well and were allowed to own property.

Many Egyptian workers were serfs. This meant that their freedom was limited. They could be bought and sold along with the estates where they worked. Farmers had to be registered with the government. They had to sell crops at a fixed price and pay taxes in the form of produce. During the season of the Nile floods, when the fields lay under water, many workers were recruited into public building projects. Punishment for those who ran away was harsh.

PLOUGHING WITH OXEN
This model figure from a tomb is ploughing the soil with oxen. The Egyptian farm workers' daily toil was hard. Unskilled peasant labourers did not own land and were paid little.

TRANSPORTING A STATUE
These workers are moving a huge stone statue on a wooden sled hauled by ropes. Many farm workers had to labour on large public building works, building dams or pyramids, each summer and autumn. Their food and lodging were provided, but they were not paid wages. Only the official classes were exempt from this service, but anyone rich enough could pay someone else to do the work for them. Slaves were used for really hard labour, such as mining and quarrying.

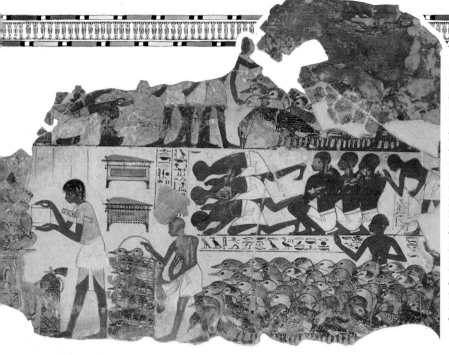

COUNTING GEESE

A farmer's flock of geese is counted out in this wall painting. Every other year, government officials visited each farm. They would count the animals to see how much tax had to be paid to the pharaoh. Taxes were paid in produce rather than money. The scribe on the left is recording this information. Scribes were members of the official classes and therefore had a higher position than other workers.

CARRYING BREAD

A woman carries a tray of loaves on her head. Most of the cooking in large houses and palaces was done by male servants, but baking bread was the job of the women. Baking was one of the few public jobs open to women.

GRINDING CORN

This model from 2325BC shows a female servant grinding wheat or barley grains into flour. She is using a stone hand-mill called a quern.

GIVE THAT MAN A BEATING

This tomb painting shows an official overseeing work in the fields. Unskilled peasant farmers were attached to an estate belonging to the pharaoh, a temple, or a rich landowner. Farmers who could not or would not give a large percentage of their harvest in rent and taxes to the pharaoh were punished harshly. They might be beaten, and their tools or their house could be seized as payment. There were law courts, judges and local magistrates in place to punish tax collectors who took bribes.

Farmers and Crops

HARVEST FESTIVAL
A priestess makes an offering of harvest produce in the tomb of Nakht. The picture shows some of the delicious fruits grown in Egypt. These included figs, grapes and pomegranates.

FARMING TOOLS
Hoes were used to break up soil that had been too heavy for the ploughs. They were also used for digging soil. The sharp sickle was used to cut grain.

sickle   *hoes*

THE ANCIENT EGYPTIANS called the banks of the Nile the Black Land because of the mud that was washed downstream each year from Central Africa. The Nile flooded in June, depositing this rich, fertile mud in Egypt. The land remained underwater until autumn.

By November the ground was ready for ploughing and then sowing. Seeds were scattered over the soil and trampled in by the hooves of sheep or goats. During the drier periods of the year, farmers dug channels and canals to bring water to irrigate their land. In the New Kingdom, a lifting system called the *shaduf* was introduced to raise water from the river. The success of this farming cycle was vital. Years of low flood or drought could spell disaster. If the crops failed, people went hungry.

Farm animals included ducks, geese, pigs, sheep and goats. Cows grazed the fringes of the desert or the greener lands of the delta region. Oxen were used for hauling ploughs and donkeys were widely used to carry goods.

TOILING IN THE FIELDS
Grain crops were usually harvested in March or April, before the great heat began. The ears of wheat or barley were cut off with a sickle made of wood and sharpened flint. In some well-irrigated areas there was a second harvest later in the summer.

MAKE A SHADUF

You will need: card, pencil, ruler, scissors, pva glue, masking tape, acrylic paint (blue, green, brown), water pot and brush, balsa wood strips, small stones, twig, clay, hessian, string .
Note: mix green paint with dried herbs for the grass mixture.

c = water tank

15cm · 5cm · 2.5cm · 3cm
5cm · 9cm · 2.5cm
23cm · 23cm · 23cm · 9cm · c · 9cm
a · 3.5cm · 2.5cm
7cm · 3.5cm
16cm · 4cm
5cm · 5c · 23cm · b · 23cm
15cm · 8cm · 23cm
a = irrigation channel & river bank · 4cm
3.5cm · 7c
b = river

Cut out the cardboard shapes (a), (b) and (c) as shown.

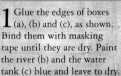

1 Glue the edges of boxes (a), (b) and (c), as shown. Bind them with masking tape until they are dry. Paint the river (b) and the water tank (c) blue and leave to dry.

HERDING THE OXEN

This New Kingdom wall painting shows oxen being herded in front of a government inspector. Cattle were already being bred along the banks of the Nile in the days before the pharaohs. They provided milk, meat and leather. They hauled wooden ploughs and were killed as sacrifices to the gods in the temples.

NILE CROPS

The chief crops were barley and wheat, used for making beer and bread. Beans and lentils were grown alongside leeks, onions, cabbages, radishes, lettuces and cucumbers. Juicy melons, dates and figs could be grown in desert oases. Grapes were grown in vineyards.

leeks   *onions*

WATERING MACHINE

The *shaduf* has a bucket on one end of a pole and a heavy weight at the other. First the weight is pushed up, lowering the bucket into the river. As the weight is lowered, it raises up the full bucket.

The mechanical lifting system called the shaduf *was invented in the Middle East. It was brought into Egypt about 3,500 years ago.*

2 Paint the river bank with the green grass mixture on top, brown on the sides and the irrigation channel blue. Next, get the balsa strips for the frame of the shaduf.

3 Glue the strips together, supporting them with masking tape and a piece of card. When dry, paint the frame brown. Glue the stones onto the water tank.

4 Use a twig for the shaduf pole. Make a weight from clay wrapped in hessian. Tie it to one end of the pole. Make a bucket from clay, leaving two holes for the string.

5 Thread the string through the bucket and tie to the pole. Tie the pole, with its weight and bucket, to the shaduf frame. Finally, glue the frame to the bank.

Food and Banquets

WORKING PEOPLE in Egypt were often paid in food. They ate bread, onions and salted fish, washed down with a sweet, grainy beer. Flour was often gritty and the teeth of many mummies show signs of severe wear and tear. Dough was kneaded with the feet or by hand, and pastry cooks produced all kinds of cakes and loaves.

BEAUTIFUL BOWLS
Dishes and bowls were often made of faience, a glassy pottery. The usual colour for this attractive tableware was blue-green or turquoise.

A big banquet for a pharaoh was a grand affair, with guests dressed in their finest clothes. A royal menu might include roast goose or stewed beef, kidneys, wild duck or tender gazelle. Lamb was not eaten for religious reasons, and in some regions certain types of fish were also forbidden. Vegetables such as leeks were stewed with milk and cheese. Egyptian cooks were experts at stewing, roasting and baking.

Red and white wines were served at banquets. They were stored in pottery jars marked with their year and their vineyard, just like the labels on modern wine bottles.

A FEAST FIT FOR A KING
New Kingdom noblewomen exchange gossip at a dinner party. They show off their jewellery and best clothes. The Egyptians loved wining and dining. They would be entertained by musicians, dancers and acrobats during the feast.

MAKE A CAKE

You will need: 200g stoneground flour, ½ tsp salt, 1tsp baking powder, 75g butter, 60g honey, 3tbsp milk, caraway seeds, bowl, wooden spoon, floured surface, baking tray.

1 Begin by mixing together the flour, salt and baking powder in the bowl. Next, chop up the butter and add it to the mixture.

2 Using your fingers, rub the butter into the mixture, as shown. Your mixture should look like fine breadcrumbs when you have finished.

3 Now add 40g of your honey. Combine it with your mixture. This will sweeten your cakes. The ancient Egyptians did not have sugar.

WOMAN MAKING BEER

This wooden tomb model of a woman making beer dates back to 2400BC. Beer was made by mashing barley bread in water. When the mixture fermented, becoming alcoholic, the liquid was strained off into a wooden tub. There were various types of beer, but all were very popular. It was said that the god Osiris had brought beer to the land of Egypt.

DRINKING VESSEL

This beautiful faience cup could have been used to drink wine, water or beer. It is decorated with a pattern of lotus flowers.

DESERT DESSERTS

An Egyptian meal could be finished off with nuts such as almonds or sweet fruits – juicy figs, dates, grapes, pomegranates or melons. Sugar was still unknown so honey was used to sweeten cakes and pastries.

pomegranates   *dates*

PALACE BAKERY

Whole teams of model cooks and bakers were left in some tombs. This was so that a pharaoh could order them to put on a good banquet to entertain his guests in the other world. Models are shown sifting, mixing and kneading flour, and making pastries. Most of our knowledge about Egyptian food and cooking comes from the food boxes and offerings left in tombs.

Egyptian pastries were often shaped in spirals like these. Other popular shapes were rings like doughnuts, and pyramids. Some were shaped like crocodiles!

4 Add the milk and stir the mixture until it forms a dough. Make your dough into a ball and place it on a floured board or surface. Divide the dough into three.

5 Roll the dough into long strips, as shown. Take the strips and coil them into a spiral to make one cake. Make the other cakes in the same way.

6 Now sprinkle each cake with caraway seeds and place them on a greased baking tray. Finish off by glazing the cakes carefully with a little extra honey.

7 Ask an adult to bake them in an oven at 180°C/Gas Mark 4 for 20 minutes. When they are ready, take them out and leave on a baking rack to cool.

Egyptian Dress

THE MOST COMMON TEXTILE in Egypt was linen. It was mostly a spotless white. Dyes such as iron (red), indigo (blue) and saffron (yellow) were sometimes used, but coloured and patterned clothes were usually the mark of a foreigner. However, the Egyptians did decorate their clothes with beads and beautiful feathers. Wool was not used for weaving in ancient Egypt. Silk and cotton did not appear until foreign rulers came to power in Egypt, after about 1000BC.

The basic items of dress for men were a simple kilt, loin-cloth or tunic. Women wore a long, closely fitting dress of fine fabric. Fashions for both men and women varied over the ages, with changes in the straps, pleating and folds.

Although more elaborate styles of clothing did appear in the New Kingdom, clothing was relatively simple, with elaborate wigs, jewellery and eye make-up creating a more dramatic effect.

LUCKY BRACELET
The bracelet above features an *udjat* eye – this eye charm was thought to protect those who carried it. Many items of jewellery featured such charms for decoration as well as for superstitious reasons. Some necklaces and earrings featured magic charms to prevent snake bites or other disasters.

GOLDEN SANDALS
These gold sandals were found in the tomb of Sheshonq II. Sandals for the rich were usually made of fine leather, while the poor used sandals made of papyrus or woven grass.

40

FABRICS

Linen was made from the plant flax. Its stalks were soaked, pounded and then rolled into lengths. The fibre was spun into thread by hand on a whirling spindle, and the thread kept moist in the mouths of the spinners. It was then ready for weaving. The first Egyptian looms were flat, but upright looms were brought in during the Hyksos period.

linen

FIT FOR A KING AND QUEEN

This panel from a golden throne shows Tutankhamun and his wife, Ankhesenamun, in their palace. The pictures are made from glass, silver, precious stones and faience (glazed pottery). The queen is wearing a long, pleated dress, while the pharaoh wears a pleated kilt. Garments were draped around the wearer rather than sewn, and pleating was very popular from the Middle Kingdom onwards. Both Tutankhamun and his wife wear sandals, bracelets, wide collars and beautiful headdresses or crowns. The queen is offering her husband perfume or ointment from a bowl.

FIRST FASHIONS

This shirt was found in the tomb of Tarkhan. It was made nearly 5,000 years ago during the reign of the pharaoh Djet. The fabric is linen and there are pleats across the shoulders.

COLOURFUL COLLARS

Wide, brilliantly coloured collars were made of glass beads, flowers, berries and leaves. They were worn for banquets and other special occasions. Collars found in Tutankhamun's tomb included those made of olive leaves and cornflowers. By examining such plants, archaeologists can find out important information about gardening, farming, the climate and insect life in ancient Egypt.

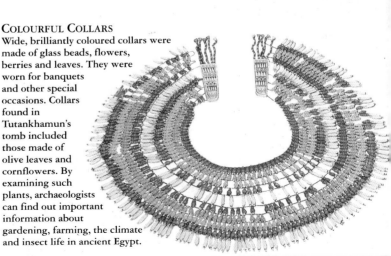

Looking Beautiful

BOTH EGYPTIAN MEN and women wore cosmetics. Their make-up included green eyeshadow made from a mineral called malachite and black eyeliner made from galena, a type of lead. Lipsticks and blusher were made from red ochre, and the early Egyptians also liked tattoos. Most Egyptian men were clean shaven. Priests also shaved their heads and the short haircut of the pharaoh was always kept covered in public. Wigs were worn by men and women, even by those who had plenty of hair of their own. Grey hair was dyed and there were various remedies for baldness. One was a lotion made from donkey's hoof, dog's paw, date stones and oil!

A TIMELESS BEAUTY
This limestone head is of Queen Nefertiti, the wife of the Sun-worshipping pharaoh Akhenaten. She seems to be the ideal of Egyptian beauty. She wears a headdress and a necklace. The stone is painted and so we can see that she is also wearing make-up and lipstick.

MIRROR, MIRROR
Mirrors were made of polished copper or bronze, with handles of wood or ivory. This bronze mirror is from 1900BC. Mirrors were used by the wealthy for checking hairstyles, applying make-up, or simply for admiring one's own good looks! The poor had to make do with seeing their reflection in water.

MAKE A MIRROR

You will need: mirror card, pencil, scissors, self-drying clay, modelling tool, rolling pin and board, small piece of card or sandpaper, gold paint, pva glue and brush, waterpot and brush.

1 Begin by drawing a mirror shape on the white side of a piece of mirror card, as shown. Carefully cut the mirror shape out. Put the card to one side.

2 Take your clay and roll it into a tube. Then mould it into a handle shape, as shown. Decorate the handle with a lotus or papyrus flower, or other design.

3 Now make a slot in the handle with a square piece of card or sandpaper, as shown. This is where the mirror card will slot into the handle.

BIG WIGS AND WAXY CONES

Many pictures show nobles at banquets wearing cones of perfumed grease on their heads. The scent may have been released as the cones melted in the heat. However, some experts believe that the cones were drawn in by artists to show that the person was wearing a scented wig. False hairpieces and wigs were very popular in Egypt. It was common for people to cut their hair short, but some did have long hair that they dressed in elaborate styles.

COSMETICS

During the early years of the Egyptian Empire, black eye kohl was made from galena, a type of poisonous lead! Later soot was used. Henna was painted on the nails and the soles of the feet to make them red. Popular beauty treatments included pumice stone to smooth rough skin and ash face packs.

face pack   *pumice stone*   *kohl*   *henna*

COSMETICS BOWL

Cosmetics, oils and lotions were prepared and stored in jars and bowls, as well as in hollow reeds or tubes. These containers were made of stone, pottery and glass. Minerals were ground into a powder and then mixed with water in cosmetics bowls to make a paste. Make-up was applied with the fingers or with a special wooden applicator. Two colours of eye make-up were commonly used – green and black. Green was used in the early period, but later the distinctive black eye paint became more popular.

The shape of mirrors and their shining surface reminded Egyptians of the Sun disc, so they became religious symbols. By the New Kingdom, many were decorated with the goddess Hathor or lotus flowers.

4 Place the handle on a wire baking tray and leave it in a warm place to dry. Turn it over after two hours. When it is completely dry, try your mirror for size.

5 It is now time to paint the handle. Paint one side carefully with gold paint and leave it to dry. When it has dried, turn the handle over and paint the other side.

6 Finally, you can assemble your mirror. Cover the base of the mirror card in glue and insert it into the handle slot. Leave it in a warm place to dry.

Papyrus and Scribes

THE WORD PAPER comes from papyrus, the reed that grows on the banks of the river Nile. To make paper, the Egyptians peeled the outer layer off the reeds. The pith inside the stems was cut into strips, soaked in water and then placed in criss-cross layers. These were hammered until they were squashed together. The surface of the papyrus was then smoothed out with a wooden tool. Other writing materials included fragments of pottery, leather and plastered boards.

It is thought that only about four out of every 1,000 Egyptians could read or write. Scribes were professional writers who would copy out official records and documents, letters, poems and stories. The training of young scribes was thorough, strict and harsh. One teacher, Amenemope, wrote to his students, "pass no day in idleness or you will be beaten". However, most workers envied the scribes for their easy way of life. They were well rewarded for their work.

EXERCISE BOOKS
School exercises were often written on broken pieces of stone or pottery that had been thrown away. These pieces are known as *ostraka*. Young scribes would copy exercises out onto the ostrakon and then have them corrected by a teacher. Many examples of corrected exercises have been discovered in Egypt.

SCRIBES RECORDING THE HARVEST
Kneeling scribes record the size of the grain harvest. The farmer would then have to give a proportion of the grain to the pharaoh as a tax. Many scribes worked in the government, copying out accounts, taxes, orders and laws. They were like civil servants.

WRITING CASE

This scribe's pen-case dates back to around 3000BC. It contains reed pens and an inkwell. The ink was made of charcoal or soot, mixed with water. Scribes carried a grinder for crushing the pigments first. Often the scribe's name and the name of his employer or the pharaoh would be carved into the case.

PENS

In ancient Egypt brushes and pens were made of reed. Blocks of ink were mixed with water on a special palette. Black ink was made from charcoal and red ink was made from ochre (an iron compound). Both were mixed with gum.

charcoal

reed pen

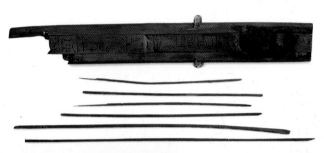

PORTABLE PALETTE

The work of a scribe often meant he had to travel on business, to record official documents. Most had a portable palette like this for when they went away. Scribes often carried a briefcase or document carrier too, to protect the information they had recorded.

FAMOUS SCRIBES

Accroupi sits cross-legged, holding a scroll of papyrus and a pen-case. Accroupi was a famous scribe who lived in Egypt at the time of the Old Kingdom. Scribes were often powerful people in ancient Egypt, and many statues of them have survived. The high standing of scribes is confirmed in the text *Satire of the Trades,* which says: "Behold! no scribe is short of food and of riches from the palace".

SYMBOL FOR A SCRIBE

The hieroglyph for a scribe is made up of a water pot, a brush holder and a palette with cakes of ink. The Egyptian word for scribe or official was *sesh*.

Ways of Writing

WE KNOW so much about the ancient Egyptians because of the written language they left behind. Inscriptions providing detailed information about their lives can be found on everything from obelisks to tombs. From about 3100BC they used pictures called hieroglyphs. Each of these could stand for an object, an idea or a sound. There were originally around 1,000 hieroglyphic symbols.

Hieroglyphs were used for thousands of years, but from 1780BC a script called hieratic was also popular. Yet another script, demotic, was used as well as hieroglyphs in the latter days of ancient Egypt.

However, by AD600, long after the last of the pharaohs, no one understood hieroglyphs. The secrets of ancient Egypt were lost for 1,200 years, until the discovery of the Rosetta Stone.

THE ROSETTA STONE
The discovery of the Rosetta Stone was a lucky accident. In 1799, a French soldier discovered a piece of stone at an Egyptian village called el-Rashid or Rosetta. On the stone, the same words were written in three scripts representing two languages. Hieroglyphic text is at the top, demotic text is in the centre, and Greek is at the bottom.

EGYPTIAN CODE CRACKED
French scholar Jean-François Champollion cracked the Rosetta Stone code in 1822. The stone contains a royal decree written in 196BC when the Greek king Ptolemy V was in power in Egypt. The Greek on the stone enabled Champollion to translate the hieroglyphs. This one discovery is central to our understanding of the way the ancient Egyptians used to live.

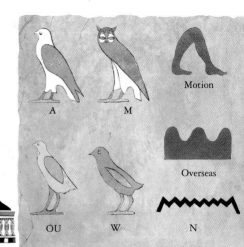

A

M

Motion

OU

W

N

Overseas

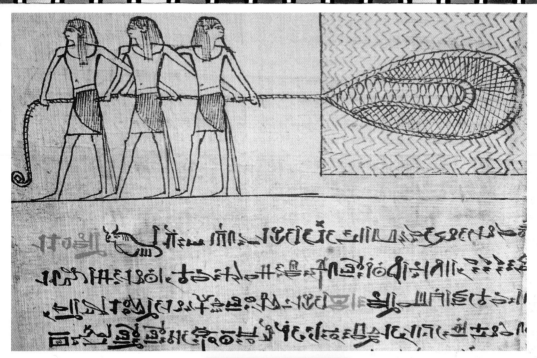

HIERATIC SCRIPT

Hieratic script (*above*) took the picture symbols of hieroglyphs and turned them into shapes that were more like letters. This script was more flowing and could be written quickly. It was used for stories, letters and business contracts. It was always read from right to left.

DEMOTIC SCRIPT

Demotic script (*left*) was introduced towards the end of the Late Kingdom. This could be written even more quickly than hieratic script. Initially it was used for business, but soon it was also being used for religious and scientific writings. It disappeared when Egypt came under Roman rule.

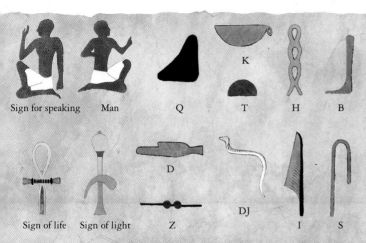

Sign for speaking   Man   Q   K   T   H   B

Sign of life   Sign of light   Z   D   DJ   I   S

HIEROGLYPHS

Hieroglyphs were made up of small pictures. These pictures were based on simplified sketches of birds and snakes, plants, parts of the body, boats and houses. Some hieroglyphs represented complete ideas such as light, travel or life. Others stood for letters or sounds that could be combined to make words.

Science and Technology

THE ANCIENT EGYPTIANS had advanced systems of numbering and measuring. They put their knowledge to good use in building, engineering and in surveying land. However, their knowledge of science was often mixed up with superstitions and belief in magic. For example, doctors understood a lot about broken bones and surgery, but at the same time they used all kinds of spells, amulets and magic potions to ward off disease. Much of their knowledge about the human body came from their experience of preparing the dead for burial.

The priests studied the stars carefully. They thought that the planets must be gods. The Egyptians also worked out a calendar, and this was very important for deciding when the Nile floods would arrive and when to plant crops.

CUBIT MEASURE
Units of measurement included the royal cubit of about 52cm and the short cubit of 45cm. A cubit was the length of a man's forearm and was subdivided into palms and fingers.

MATHEMATICAL PAPYRUS
This papyrus shows methods for working out the areas of squares, circles and triangles. It dates from around 850BC. These methods would have been used in calculations for land areas and pyramid heights on Egyptian building projects. Other surviving Egyptian writings show mathematical calculations to work out how much grain would fit into a store. The Egyptians used a decimal system of numbering with separate symbols for one, ten, 100 and 1,000. Eight was shown by eight one symbols – 11111111.

MAKE A WATER CLOCK

You will need: self-drying clay, plastic flowerpot, modelling tool, skewer, pencil, ruler, masking tape, scissors, yellow acrylic paint , varnish, water pot and brush. Optional: rolling pin and board.

1 Begin by rolling out the clay. Take the plastic flowerpot and press its base firmly into the clay. This will be the bottom of your water clock.

2 Cut out an oblong of clay large enough to mould around the flowerpot. Add the base and use your modelling tool to make the joints smooth.

3 Make a small hole near the bottom of the pot with a skewer, as shown. Leave the pot in a warm place to dry. When the clay has dried, remove the flowerpot.

NILOMETER

A series of steps called a Nilometer was used to measure the depth of the water in the river Nile. The annual floods were desperately important for the farmers living alongside the Nile.
A good flood measured about 7m. More than this and farm buildings and channels might be destroyed. Less than this and the fields might go dry.

MEDICINE

Most Egyptian medicines were based on plants. One cure for headaches included juniper berries, coriander, wormwood and honey. The mixture was rubbed into the scalp. Other remedies included natron (a kind of salt), myrrh and even crocodile droppings. Some Egyptian medicines probably did heal the patients, but others did more harm than good.

coriander

garlic

STAR OF THE NILE

This astronomical painting is from the ceiling of the tomb of Seti I. The study of the stars was part religion, part science. The brightest star in the sky was Sirius, which we call the dog star. The Egyptians called it Sopdet, after a goddess. This star rose into view at the time when the Nile floods were due and was greeted with a special festival.

4 Mark out lines at 3mm intervals inside the pot. Mask the ends with tape and paint the lines yellow. When dry, remove the tape. Ask an adult to varnish the pot inside.

5 Find or make another two pots and position them as shown. Ask a partner to put their finger over the hole in the clock while you pour water into it.

6 Now ask your partner to take their finger away. The length of time it takes for the level of the water to drop from mark to mark is the measure of time.

Time was calculated on water clocks by calculating how long it took for water to drop from level to level. The water level lowered as it dripped through the hole in the bottom of the pot.

Music and Dance

ALTHOUGH MUCH OF OUR KNOWLEDGE about the Egyptians comes from their interest in death, they also loved life. Paintings show how much they enjoyed dancing and music. Also, many musical instruments have been found inside tombs. Music was played for pleasure and entertainment, as well as for religious worship and for marching into battle.

The first Egyptian instruments were probably flutes and harps. Instruments similar to pipes, oboes and trumpets later became popular. During the New

Kingdom, lutes and lyres were brought in from Asia. Bells, cymbals, tambourines and drums kept the beat, along with a sacred rattle called the sistrum.

Dancers performed at banquets, sometimes doing acrobatic feats in time to the music. Other dances were more solemn, being performed in temples and at funerals.

THE SISTRUM
A priestess is rattling a sistrum. The ancient Egyptians called this instrument a *seshesht*. It is made of a loop of bronze containing loose rods that rattled when shaken.

STRING SOUNDS
Musicians play a harp, a lyre and a lute at a banquet. These were among the most common string instruments in ancient Egypt. During the New Kingdom female musicians became very popular.

MAKE A RATTLE

You will need: self-drying clay, balsa wood (1.5 x 15cm), card, modelling tool, skewer, wire and 10 washers, pliers, pva glue and brush, acrylic paint (brown or red and black mixed, gold), water pot and brush.

1 For the handle, you will need the block of clay and the balsa wood. Push the balsa wood into the square block of clay to make a hole for the handle.

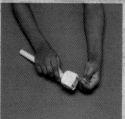

2 Next, make two slots in the top of the clay block for the card part of the rattle to fit into. The card will form the shaker part of the sistrum.

3 Sculpt the face of the goddess Hathor into the top of the handle. Look at the picture of her on page 12. Now leave the clay in a warm place to dry.

MUSICIANS OF THEBES

This famous wall painting from Thebes is about 3,400 years old. It shows women dancers and musicians performing at a banquet. The Egyptians tended to listen to professional musicians rather than play for their own pleasure. No Egyptian music was written down, but we do still know the words of some of their songs. The hieroglyphs above this picture tell us that the musicians are playing a song in praise of nature. The dancing girls in the painting shake their bodies gracefully to the rhythm of the music.

HARPIST

A male harpist plays a hymn to the god Horus. The first Egyptian harps were plain and simple, but later they were beautifully made, carved and painted gold.

4 Pierce two holes into the card. Thread the wire through the washers and then through the holes in the card. Bend the wire back with pliers to secure it.

5 Push the head of the rattle into the slots in the handle and then glue into position. Paint the rattle brown and rub in gold paint to create a bronze look.

The sistrum was a sacred rattle used by noblewomen and priestesses at religious ceremonies and musical festivities. It was used in the worship of Hathor, the goddess of love.

Entertainment and Leisure

ONE OF THE FAVOURITE PASTIMES of the Egyptians was hunting. They hunted for pleasure as well as for food, using bows and arrows, throwing sticks, spears and nets. Thousands of years ago, many wild animals lived in Egypt. Today most of these are found only in lands far to the south. They included hippopotamuses and lions. Hunting these animals was extremely dangerous, and pictures show the pharaoh setting out bravely for the hunt. In practice the animals were often trapped and released into an enclosure before the pharaoh arrived. There he could easily catch them from the safety of his chariot.

ANIMAL CHAMPIONS
Here the lion and the antelope, two old enemies, are sitting down peacefully for a game of *senet*. This painting dates from about 1150BC. *Senet* could be played on fine boards or on simple grids scratched on stones or drawn in sand.

Chariots first appeared in Egypt during the Hyksos period, and racing them soon became a fashionable sport with the nobles. One sport that was popular with all Egyptians was wrestling. There was no theatre in Egypt, but storytellers at the royal court and on village streets told fables and stories about battles, gods and magic.

Board games were popular from the early days of Egypt. In the tomb of Tutankhamun there was a beautiful gaming board made of ebony and ivory, designed for two games called *senet* and *tjau*.

YOUR MOVE
This noble is playing *senet*, eagerly watched by his wife. The players threw dice to decide how many squares to move over at one time. Some of the squares had forfeits and some had gains. *Senet* was said to be a game of struggle against evil.

MAKE A MEHEN BOARD
You will need: self-drying clay, rolling pin and board, ruler, modelling tool, green paint, cloth, varnish, water pot and brush. For the game: 12 round counters 6 blue on one side/grey on the other, 6 gold on one side/orange on the other, 2 larger counters, dice.

1 Roll out the clay onto the board and cut it to the shape shown. Use the ruler and modelling tool to score on the lines of the snake at regular intervals. Leave to dry.

2 Next, rub the board with diluted green paint to stain the lines. Wipe the excess paint away with a rag. Leave it to dry. Finally, ask an adult to varnish it.

3 Each player has 6 counters of the same colours plus a larger piece (the lion). Turn all your counters so they show the same colour. You need to throw a one to start each counter off.

THE LAST GAME

This gaming board comes from Tutankhamun's tomb. Board games were so popular that they were placed in tombs to offer the dead person some fun in the next life.

HOLDS AND THROWS

Wrestling was one sport that any Egyptian could do. It did not need expensive chariots or any other special equipment. It was popular with rich and poor alike.

WILDFOWLING IN THE MARSHES

Nebamun, a nobleman, is enjoying a day's wildfowling in the marshes of the Nile Delta. He stands in his reed boat and hurls a throwing stick, a kind of boomerang, at the birds flying out of the reeds. His cat already seems to have caught several birds.

Mehen, *the snake game, was popular in Egypt before* 3000BC.

4 You must start each of your counters on the board before advancing any of the others. A throw of one ends a go and allows your opponent to take their turn.

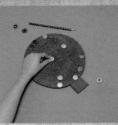

5 Exact numbers are needed to reach the centre. Once at the centre, turn your counter over to start its return journey. When it has got back to the start, your lion piece can begin.

6 The lion moves to the centre in the same way as the other counters. However, on its return journey, it can eat any of your opponent's counters in its way.

7 The winner is the person whose lion has eaten the largest number of counters. Work out the number of counters you got home safely and see who has the most left.

A Child's World

ALTHOUGH EGYPTIAN CHILDREN had only a brief period of childhood before education and work, they did enjoy playing with rattles, balls, spinning tops, toy horses and toy crocodiles. They wrestled in the dust, ran races and swam in the river.

Girls from ordinary Egyptian families received little schooling. They were taught how to look after the household, how to spin, weave and cook. When girls grew up there were few jobs open to them, although they did have legal rights and some noblewomen became very powerful. Boys were mostly trained to do the same jobs as their fathers. Some went to scribe school, where they learned how to read and write. Slow learners were beaten without mercy. Boys and some girls from noble families received a broader education, learning how to read, write and do sums.

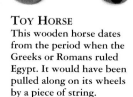

TOY HORSE
This wooden horse dates from the period when the Greeks or Romans ruled Egypt. It would have been pulled along on its wheels by a piece of string.

FUN FOR ALL
Spinning tops were popular toys with children in Egypt. They were made of glazed stone and would have been cheap enough for poorer families to buy.

ISIS AND HORUS
Many statues show the goddess Isis with Horus as a child sitting on his mother's lap. The young Horus was believed to protect families from danger and accidents. The Egyptians had large families and family life was important to them.

A LION THAT ROARS
You will need: self-drying clay, rolling pin and board, modelling tool, a piece of card, skewer, balsa wood, sandpaper, acrylic paint (white, green, red, blue, black, yellow), masking tape, string, water pot & brush.

1 Begin by rolling out the clay. Cut the pieces to the shapes shown. Mould the legs onto the body and the base. Put the bottom jaw piece to one side.

2 Use your modelling tool to make a hole between the lion's upper body and the base, as shown. This hole is for the lower jaw to fit into.

3 Insert the lower jaw into the hole you have just made and prop it up with a piece of card. Make a hole through the upper and lower jaws with the skewer.

THE LOCK OF YOUTH

When they were young, boys and girls wore a special haircut, a shaved head with a lock of plaited hair. This plait, or lock of youth, was allowed to grow over one side of children's faces. When they reached adulthood, many Egyptians would have their heads shaved and wear an elaborate wig.

BOUNCING BACK

Egyptian children enjoyed playing games with balls made from rags, linen and reeds. However, archaeologists are not certain whether the balls above were used for the playing of games or as a type of rattle for younger children.

Originally this toy would have been made of wood, with a bronze tooth.

A TOY LION

Pull the string, and the lion roars! Or is it a cat miaowing? Children once played with this animal on the banks of the Nile. At the time, this toy would have been brightly painted.

4 Now use the skewer to make a hole from left to right through the lion's upper body. The string will go through these holes later to be connected to the jaw.

5 Push a small piece of balsa wood into the mouth. This will form the lion's tooth. Leave the clay lion to dry and then sand down the surface.

6 Paint the lion in white, yellow, blue, black and red, as shown. Use masking tape to ensure that your lines are straight. Leave the lion in a warm place to dry.

7 Thread the string through the holes in the upper body and tie it to secure. A second string then goes through the lower and upper jaws of your lion.

Weapons and Warriors

EGYPT was surrounded by harsh deserts on three sides. In the north were the marshes of the delta and to the south the Nile ran over a series of rapids and waterfalls, the cataracts. All these formed barriers to invading armies. Even so, Egyptian towns were defended with forts and walls, and many pharaohs went into battle against their neighbours. Wars were fought against the Libyans, the Nubians, the Hittites and the Syrians.

There were professional soldiers in Egypt, but most were forced to join the army. For slaves, fighting in the army was a chance to gain their freedom. At times, foreign troops were also hired to fight. Young men in the villages learned to drill in preparation for war. Soldiers carried shields of leather and wood. They were armed with spears, axes, bows and arrows, daggers and swords. Later, war chariots drawn by horses were used. Special awards, such as the golden fly, were handed out for bravery in battle.

KING DEN
This ivory label from 3000BC shows King Den striding into battle against an eastern enemy. He stands beneath the flag, or standard, of the jackal-headed god Anubis. He is armed with a club, or mace.

RIDING TO VICTORY
Egyptian art often shows scenes of a pharaoh riding into battle or returning home in triumph. The king is shown in a fine chariot, driving prisoners before him. Artists often showed the enemy as very small, to show the importance and power of the pharaoh. This plaque of red gold shows Tutankhamun as the all-conquering hero.

MAKE A GOLDEN FLY

You will need: card, pencil, ruler, scissors, self-drying clay, pva glue and brush, acrylic paint (gold), gold or white ribbon (40cm long x 1cm wide), water pot and brush.

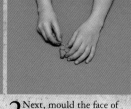

1 Begin by making the body and wings of the fly. Use a ruler and pencil to draw the fly shape onto the card, as shown. Then cut it out carefully with scissors.

2 Next, mould the face of the fly in clay. Roll two small balls for the eyes and outline them with coils of clay. This will make the eyes look larger.

3 Take the card, bend over the tab and glue it down, as shown. This will make a loop. When the fly is finished, ribbon will be threaded through this loop.

BATTLE AXE

This axe has a silver handle and a long blade designed to give a slicing movement. The battle axe was the Egyptian foot soldiers' favourite weapon. Its head of copper or bronze was fitted into a socket or lashed to the wooden handle with leather thongs. Soldiers did not wear armour in battle. Their only protection against weapons such as the heavy axes and spears was large shields made of wood or leather. The mummy of the pharaoh Seqenenre Tao shows terrible wounds to the skull caused by an axe, a dagger and a spear on the battlefield.

DAGGERS

These ceremonial daggers were found in Tutankhamun's tomb. They are similar to those that would have been used in battle. Egyptian daggers were short and fairly broad. The blades were made of copper or bronze. An iron dagger was also found in Tutankhamun's tomb, but this was very rare. It may have been a gift from the Hittite people, who were mastering the new skill of ironworking.

The Order of the Golden Fly was a reward for brave soldiers. This is a model of an award given to Queen Aahotep for her part in the war against the Hyksos.

4 Glue four small strips of white card onto the face, as shown. Push them into the modelling clay. Leave the fly's face in a warm place to dry.

5 Now glue the completed clay fly in place on the card wings. Leave the finished fly to dry for 20 minutes or so before painting it.

6 Carefully paint the fly gold. If your ribbon is white, paint that gold too. Leave the fly and, if necessary, the ribbon to dry. Make two other flies in the same way.

7 Thread the ribbon through the loops in your golden flies, as shown. Originally the golden flies would have been worn on a chain.

Boats and Ships

THE EGYPTIANS were not great seafarers. Their ocean-going ships did sail the Red Sea and the Mediterranean, and may even have reached India, but they mostly kept to coastal waters. However, the Egyptians were experts at river travel, as they are today. They built simple boats from papyrus reed, and these were used for fishing and hunting.

Egypt had little timber, so wooden ships were often built from cedar imported from Lebanon. Boats and model ships were often placed in tombs, and archaeologists have found many well-preserved examples.

The Nile was Egypt's main road, and all kinds of boats travelled up and down. There were barges transporting stones to building sites, ferries taking people across the river, and royal pleasure boats.

THE FINAL VOYAGE
Ships often appear in Egyptian pictures. They were important symbols of the voyage to the next world after death.

ALL ALONG THE NILE
Wooden sailing ships with graceful, triangular sails can still be seen on the river Nile today. They carry goods and people up and down the river. The design of these boats, or *feluccas*, has changed since the time of the ancient Egyptians. The sails on their early boats were tall, upright and narrow. Later designs were broader, like the ones shown above. In Egypt, big towns and cities have always been built along the river, so the Nile has served as an important highway.

MAKE A BOAT

You will need: a large bundle of straw 30cm long, scissors, string, balsa wood, red and yellow card, pva glue and brush.

1 Divide the straw into five equal bundles and then cut three of them down to 15cm in length. Tie all five bundles securely at both ends and in the middle, as shown.

2 Take the two long bundles and tie them together at one end as shown. These bundles will form the outer frame of the boat. Put them to one side.

3 Next take the three short bundles of straw and bind them together at both ends. These will form the inner surface of the straw boat.

STEERING ROUND SAND BANKS

This wooden tomb model shows a boat from 1800BC with high curved ends. Long steering oars kept the boat on course through the powerful currents of the flooding river. Although timber was the main material for building larger boats, their designs were similar to those of the simple reed vessels.

SAILING TO ABYDOS

These boats are making a pilgrimage to Abydos. This was the city of Osiris, the god of death and rebirth. Mummies were taken here by boat. Ships and boats played a major part in the religious beliefs of the Egyptians. Ra the Sun god travelled on a boat across the sky. In October 1991, a fleet of 12 boats dating from about 3000BC was found at Abydos near Memphis. The boats were up to 30m in length and had been buried beneath the desert sands. The vessels found in these pits are the oldest surviving large ships in the world.

SIGN OF THE NORTH

The hieroglyph below means boat. It looks a bit like the papyrus reed vessels with their curved ends. This sign later came to mean north. A ship without a sail would always travel north with the current of the Nile.

Early boats were made from papyrus reeds. These were bound with string made from reed fibres.

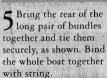

4 Next push the short bundles into the centre of the long pair firmly. Tie the bundles together with string at one end, as shown.

5 Bring the rear of the long pair of bundles together and tie them securely, as shown. Bind the whole boat together with string.

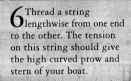

6 Thread a string lengthwise from one end to the other. The tension on this string should give the high curved prow and stern of your boat.

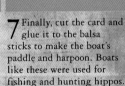

7 Finally, cut the card and glue it to the balsa sticks to make the boat's paddle and harpoon. Boats like these were used for fishing and hunting hippos.

Trade and Conquest

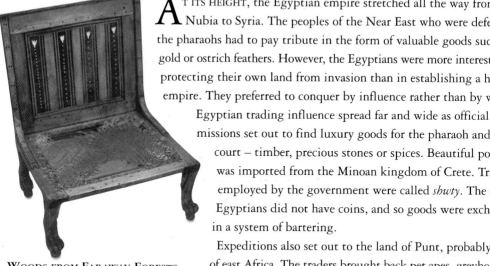

A**T ITS HEIGHT**, the Egyptian empire stretched all the way from Nubia to Syria. The peoples of the Near East who were defeated by the pharaohs had to pay tribute in the form of valuable goods such as gold or ostrich feathers. However, the Egyptians were more interested in protecting their own land from invasion than in establishing a huge empire. They preferred to conquer by influence rather than by war.

Egyptian trading influence spread far and wide as official missions set out to find luxury goods for the pharaoh and his court – timber, precious stones or spices. Beautiful pottery was imported from the Minoan kingdom of Crete. Traders employed by the government were called *shwty*. The ancient Egyptians did not have coins, and so goods were exchanged in a system of bartering.

Expeditions also set out to the land of Punt, probably a part of east Africa. The traders brought back pet apes, greyhounds, gold, ivory, ebony and myrrh. Queen Hatshepsut particularly encouraged these trading expeditions. The walls of her mortuary temple record details of them and also show a picture of Eti, the Queen of Punt.

WOODS FROM FARAWAY FORESTS
Few trees grew in Egypt, so timber for making fine furniture had to be imported. Cedarwood came from Lebanon and hardwoods such as ebony from Africa.

ALL THE RICHES OF PUNT
Sailors load a wooden sailing boat with storage jars, plants, spices and apes from the land of Punt. Goods would have been exchanged in Punt for these items. Egyptian trading expeditions travelled to many distant lands and brought back precious goods to the pharaoh. This drawing is copied from the walls of Hatshepsut's temple at Deir el-Bahri.

SYRIAN ENVOYS

Foreign rulers from Asia and the Mediterranean lands would send splendid gifts to the pharaoh, and he would send them gifts in return. These Syrians have been sent as representatives of their ruler, or envoys. They have brought perfume containers made of gold, ivory and a beautiful stone called lapis lazuli. The vases are decorated with gold and lotus flower designs. The pharaoh would pass on some of the luxurious foreign gifts to his favourite courtiers.

NUBIANS BRINGING TRIBUTE

Nubians bring goods to the pharaoh Thutmose IV – gold rings, apes and leopard skins. Nubia was the land above the Nile cataracts (rapids), now known as northern Sudan. The Egyptians acquired much of their wealth from Nubia through military campaigns. During times of peace, however, they also traded with the princes of Nubia for minerals and exotic animals.

EXOTIC GOODS

Egyptian craftsmen had to import many of their most valuable materials from abroad. These included gold, elephant tusks (for ivory), hardwoods such as ebony and softwoods such as cedar of Lebanon. Copper was mined in Nubia and bronze (a mixture of copper and tin) was imported from Syria.

ivory

ebony

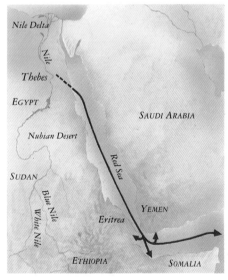

A WORLD OF TRADE

The Egyptians travelled over the Red Sea to the mysterious land of Punt. This modern map shows the voyage the traders would have made. No one is sure of the exact location of Punt, but it was probably present-day Somalia, Eritrea, Yemen or southern Sudan.

Glossary

A

amulet

alabaster A gleaming white stone, a type of gypsum.
amethyst A purple crystal, a type of quartz.
amulet A lucky charm.
artefact An object that has been preserved from the past.

C

canopic jar A pottery jar used to hold the lungs, liver, intestines and stomach of a dead person.
cataract Waterfalls or white-water rapids.
chariot A horse-drawn cart, used for warfare or racing.

chariot

civilization A society that makes advances in arts, sciences, technology, law or government.
conscript Someone who is called up by the government to serve in the army.
cosmetics Make-up.
crook and flail A hooked stick and a jointed stick, sacred to the god Osiris. The pharaohs carried the crook and flail as symbols of royal authority.
cubit A unit of measurement, the length of a forearm.

D

delta A coastal region where a river splits into separate waterways before flowing into the sea.

demotic A simplified script used in the later periods of ancient Egypt.
drought A long, dry period without rainfall.
dynasty A royal family, or the period it remains in power.

E

embalm To preserve a dead body.
empire A number of different lands coming under the rule of a single government.

F

faience A type of opaque glass that is often blue or green. It is made from quartz or sand, lime, ash and natron.
flax A blue-flowered plant grown for its fibre, which is used to make linen. It also has seeds that produce linseed oil.
furl To roll up the sail of a ship.

faience china

G

gazelle A small, graceful antelope.
golden fly A badge given as a reward to soldiers for bravery in battle.
grid pattern A plan dividing towns into blocks and straight streets at right angles.

H

henna A reddish dye for the hair or skin, made from the leaves of a shrub.
hieratic A shorthand version of hieroglyphic script, used by priests.

hieroglyph A picture symbol used in ancient Egyptian writing.
Hyksos A people from the region of Palestine, who settled in Egypt after 1800BC and ruled the country.

Hyksos

I

incense Sweet-smelling gum or bark burnt as part of religious ceremonies.
indigo A dark blue dye taken from plants.
irrigate To bring water to dry land.

J

jackal A wild dog that lives in Asia and Africa.

L

loom A frame on which cloth is woven.
Lower Egypt The northern part of Egypt, especially the Nile delta.
lute A string musical instrument.
lyre A harp-like musical instrument.

M

Middle Kingdom The period of Egyptian history between 2050 and 1786BC.
mummy A human, or sometimes animal, body preserved by drying.

N

natron Salty crystals used in preparing mummies.
Nekhbet The name of the vulture goddess.
New Kingdom The period of Egyptian history between 1550–1070BC.
Nilometer A series of measured steps or a column used to measure the depth of the Nile floods.

O

oasis A place where there is water in a desert area.
obelisk A pointed pillar, erected as a monument.
ochre A red or yellow earth.
Old Kingdom The period of Egyptian history between 2686 and 2181BC.

obelisk

P

papyrus A tall reedy plant that grows in the river Nile. It is used for making paper.
pendant A piece of jewellery hung on a chain around the neck.
pharaoh The ruler of ancient Egypt.
pigment Any colouring used to make paint.

the pharaoh Thutmose III

potter's wheel A round slab, spun round to help shape the wet clay when making pots by hand.
prow The front end of a ship.

pyramid A large pointed monument with a broad, square base and triangular sides.

R

ritual A ceremony that is often religious.

S

saffron An orange spice and dye, taken from crocuses.
sarcophagus The stone casing for a coffin.
sceptre A rod carried by a king, queen or emperor as an emblem of rule.
scribe A professional writer, a clerk or civil servant.
script A method of writing.
serfs People who are not free to move from the land they farm without the permission of their lord.
shaduf A bucket on a weighted pole, used to move water from the river Nile into the fields on the banks.
shrine A container of holy relics, a place for worship.
side lock A plait of hair worn by children in ancient Egypt.
sistrum A metal rattle, used as a musical instrument in ancient Egypt.

a sistrum

sphinx The statue of a mythical creature, half lion, half human.
spindle A rod used to twist fibres into yarn while spinning.

stern The rear end of a ship.
strike A work stoppage, part of a demand for better conditions.
superstition An illogical belief in good luck or bad luck.
survey To measure land or buildings.

T

tax Goods, money or services paid to the government.
textile Any cloth produced by the process of weaving.
tribute Goods given by a country to its conquerors, as a mark of submission.
turquoise A blue-green stone.

U

Upper Egypt The southern part of Egypt.

V

Vizier The treasurer or highest-ranking official in the Egyptian court.

wildfowling

W

wildfowling Hunting wild ducks, geese and other water birds using throw sticks.

Index